AN EVOLVING ASEAN
VISION AND REALITY

Edited by Jayant Menon and Cassey Lee

SEPTEMBER 2019

ASIAN DEVELOPMENT BANK

© 2019 Asian Development Bank
6 ADB Avenue, Mandaluyong City, 1550 Metro Manila, Philippines
Tel +63 2 632 4444; Fax +63 2 636 2444
www.adb.org

Some rights reserved. Published in 2019.

ISBN 978-92-9261-694-6 (print), 978-92-9261-695-3 (electronic)
Publication Stock No. TCS199043
DOI: http://dx.doi.org/10.22617/TCS199043

Notes:
In this publication, "$" refers to United States dollars.
ADB recognizes "China" as the People's Republic of China, "Korea" as the Republic of Korea, and "Hanoi" as Ha Noi.

On the cover: Indonesia signed the ASEAN Declaration with Malaysia, the Philippines, Singapore, and Thailand in 1967 (photo from the ASEAN Secretariat Photo Archives).

This book is dedicated to former Ambassador
and ASEAN Secretary-General Rodolfo C. Severino.
27 April 1936–19 April 2019

CONTENTS

TABLES AND FIGURES

FIGURES

FOREWORD

Although the formation of the Association of Southeast Asian Nations (ASEAN) in the 1960s was originally driven by political and security concerns, ASEAN's ambit has evolved over the decades to include an ambitious and progressive economic agenda. Early attempts at economic cooperation among ASEAN member states included the adoption of the ASEAN Industrial Projects, the Agreement on ASEAN Preferential Trading Arrangements, the ASEAN Industrial Complementation scheme, and the ASEAN Industrial Joint Ventures in the 1970s and 1980s. The results from these ventures were mixed, perhaps reflecting the fact that ASEAN was not yet ready for effective trade liberalization and economic integration at that time.

In 1992, ASEAN took another bold step and adopted the Common Effective Preferential Tariff scheme under the ASEAN Free Trade Area. This solidified the foundation for ASEAN economic cooperation and spurred the adoption of more ambitious initiatives such as the ASEAN Framework Agreement on Services in 1995 and the ASEAN Investment Area in 1998. All of these efforts eventually culminated in a vision to create the ASEAN Economic Community (AEC) by 2015.

Despite recognized shortfalls in implementation in some areas, ASEAN formally launched the AEC in December 2015. With the discourse now having shifted to the vision and direction for ASEAN 2025, it is timely to reflect on the past and future of ASEAN regional economic integration. What has ASEAN already achieved, and how? Is the AEC headed in the right direction? And, more importantly, can it do a better job of binding ASEAN member states to their commitments?

To address these questions, the Asian Development Bank (ADB) and ISEAS–Yusof Ishak Institute convened the High-Level Workshop on the Evolving Nature of ASEAN's Economic Cooperation: Original Vision and Current Practice. ADB and ISEAS invited renowned economists and diplomats in the ASEAN region, many of whom were instrumental in the evolution of ASEAN's economic agenda. This volume is a compilation of the papers presented at the workshop, containing the authors' personal reflections on ASEAN's journey toward economic integration. The papers review the historical evolution of ASEAN's economic agenda, capture its achievements, examine the challenges that have surfaced in the last decade, and recommend a way forward. The papers in this volume emphasize that, while there have been notable successes, the remaining challenges suggest that ASEAN is still on its transition path in achieving full economic integration.

This volume has benefited immensely from the efforts and contributions of several people. We gratefully acknowledge the support of ISEAS-Yusof Ishak Institute, which was actively involved in coming up with the initial concept, provided financial and other support for the workshop, and assisted in preparing the manuscript for publication. We also wish to express our deep appreciation to the authors for their enthusiasm and tireless commitment to this endeavor. Finally, we wish to thank the excellent team of reviewers and editors who worked on this volume and provided much-needed guidance.

Yasuyuki Sawada
Chief Economist and Director General
Economic Research and Regional Cooperation Department
ADB

ABOUT THE EDITORS

Cassey Lee is a senior fellow and co-coordinator of the Malaysia Studies Programme at the ISEAS-Yusof Ishak Institute, Singapore. Prior to joining ISEAS, he held academic appointments at the University of Wollongong, Nottingham University Business School, and University of Malaya. Lee received his PhD in economics from University of California, Irvine. Lee specializes in industrial organization. His current research interests include algorithmic pricing, political economy of development, structural change and deindustrialization, institutional economics, and competition policy. He has published in peer-reviewed journals and is currently the co-managing editor for the *Journal of Southeast Asian Economies* and associate editor for the *Journal of Economic Surveys.*

Jayant Menon is a lead economist at the Asian Development Bank (ADB), in Manila, Philippines, where he works on trade, international investment, and development issues. He holds adjunct appointments with the Australian National University of Canberra, Australia; University of Nottingham, England; and the Institute for Democracy and Economic Affairs (IDEAS), Malaysia. He has served as a board director of the Cambodia Development Resource Institute and on the Advisory Board of the University of Nottingham Campus in Malaysia. Prior to joining ADB, he worked as an academic in Australia for more than a decade, mainly at the Center of Policy Studies at Monash University in Melbourne, Australia. He has also worked at the University of Melbourne, Victoria University, and the American University in Washington, DC. He has authored and co-authored more than a hundred academic publications, mostly on trade and development, particularly related to Asia. He holds a PhD in economics from the University of Melbourne, Australia.

ABOUT THE CONTRIBUTORS

Narongchai Akrasanee is a Thai academic and businessperson who has been at the helm of 20 different companies. He currently serves as the chairperson of the Seranee Group of companies. He is also the vice-chairperson of the Council of Mekong Institute and the chairperson of the Khon Kaen University Council in Thailand. Akrasanee was previously a member of the National Legislative Assembly. He has been an economic adviser to several Thai prime ministers and was formerly the minister of commerce and minister of energy of Thailand. He also served as chairperson of the Export–Import Bank of Thailand from December 2005 to June 2010, as director of the Office of the Insurance Commission of Thailand from October 2007 to August 2012, and as director of the National Economic and Social Development from July 2009 to July 2013. He was a member of the Monetary Policy Committee of the Bank of Thailand from November 2011 to September 2014. He was also a member of the original ASEAN Economic Research Unit at the ISEAS-Yusof Ishak Institute during its inception years. Akrasanee holds a PhD in economics and a master of arts degree in economics from John Hopkins University and a bachelor's degree in economics (Hons) from the University of Western Australia.

Delia Domingo Albert is the first woman career diplomat to become secretary (minister) of foreign affairs in the Philippines and in Asia. She represented the Philippines in Switzerland, Romania, Hungary, Germany, and Australia. Albert is a member of the advisory board of the Global Economic Symposium (GES) of Kiel University, Germany; the Institute for Cultural Diplomacy in Berlin; the Asian Institute of Management; the Ramon Magsaysay Award Foundation; the Global Summit of Women, and the International Women's Forum. She is the founding chair of Business and Professional Women Philippines (BPW-Makati chapter) and Diwata: Women in Resource Development. She attended the University of the Philippines, the Institute of International Studies in Geneva, the Diplomatic Institute in Salzburg, Boston University Overseas in Bonn, and the John Kennedy School of Government at Harvard University.

Florian Alburo is the president of the Center for the Advancement of Trade Integration and Facilitation (CATIF); a professorial lecturer of economics at the University of the Philippines in Diliman, Quezon City; a team leader at the European Union Trade-Related Technical Assistance Project; a fellow at the Center for Internet Studies of the Institute for International Policy at the University of Washington in Seattle, Washington, US; and an advisor on Trade Facilitation of the Asia-Pacific Research and Training Network on Trade (ARTNeT), United Nations Economic and Social Commission for Asia and the Pacific (UNESCAP) in Thailand. His previous experiences include being the deputy minister of socioeconomic planning and deputy director-general of the National Economic and Development Authority; a trade specialist of the Greater Mekong Subregion Cooperation Programme of ADB; a team leader for Development Alternatives, Inc.; and a team leader for the United Nations Development Programme, among others. Alburo has written for professional journals, opinion pages of newspapers, and edited publications, singly or in collaboration with economists, sociologists, and other social scientists. He has a PhD and a master of arts degree in economics from the University of Colorado, Boulder, US.

Siow Yue Chia is Senior Research Fellow at the Singapore Institute of International Affairs. She was formerly the director of the ISEAS–Yusof Ishak Institute; director of the Singapore APEC Study Centre; founding regional coordinator of the East Asian Development Network; and a professor of economics at the National University of Singapore. She has been a consultant to the World Bank, the United Nations Conference for Trade and Development, the World Trade Organization, the United Nations Economic and Social Commission for Asia and the Pacific, ADB, the Asian Development Bank Institute, the ASEAN Secretariat, and the Economic Research Institute for ASEAN and East Asia. Her research and publications cover international trade and investment, international labor mobility, and regional economic integration, with focus on Asia and the Pacific, East Asia, Southeast Asia, and Singapore. She obtained her undergraduate degrees from Singapore and PhD in economics from McGill University (Canada), specializing on international and development economics.

Emil Salim started his professional career as a lecturer with the Faculty of Economics at the Universitas Indonesia in 1956 and has been a professor since 1975. He was the vice-chairperson of the National Development Planning Agency and concurrently state minister for state apparatus reform and minister for transportation, communication and tourism from 1973 to 1978; minister for development monitoring and the environment from 1978 to 1983; and minister for population and the environment from 1988 to 1998. He is the founder and the first chairperson of the Indonesian Biodiversity Foundation (KEHATI). He was also the chairperson of the Advisory Council to the President of Indonesia. He also chaired the Foundation for Sustainable Development and cochaired the United States–Indonesia Society. Salim is member of the Indonesian Academy of Sciences. He graduated with a PhD in economics from the University of California, Berkeley, US.

Chayut Setboonsarng is a correspondent for Reuters covering business, investment, and politics. He was previously a consultant to APCO Worldwide and was part of a team that organized the unveiling of equity crowdfunding in Thailand. He was also a policy analyst at the CIMB ASEAN Research Institute. He earned his bachelor of arts degree in international studies from the University of Washington and master of arts degree in international trade and investment policy from George Washington University.

Suthad Setboonsarng has been independent director of the Somboon Advance Technology Public Company Ltd. since 2018. He serves as a board member of the Bank of Thailand and Banpu PLC, one of the largest private energy companies in Thailand. He is also a board member of the Cambodia Development Resource Institute. His prior experiences include being a consultant to the National ASEAN Summit Committee, Brunei Darussalam; a senior advisor for BowerGroupAsia, US; a Thailand trade representative (a ministerial representative of the Thai prime minister); a partner, Worldtrade Management Services, Price Waterhouse Coopers, Thailand; a deputy secretary-general of the ASEAN (Operations) Secretariat, Indonesia; an associate professor, Asian Institute of Technology, Pathumthani, Thailand; a research fellow, Thailand Development Research Institute (TDRI); a research fellow, East-West Resource System Institute, Hawaii, US; and a lecturer with the Faculty of Economics at Thammasat University, Thailand. Setboonsarng received his bachelor of arts degree in economics from the Thammasat University in Thailand and master of arts degree in agricultural economics from the University of Hawaii. He completed his PhD in economics at the University of Hawaii under a scholarship from the East–West Center, Hawaii.

Rodolfo C. Severino was an associate senior fellow at the ISEAS-Yusof Ishak Institute. He led and served as the founding head of the ASEAN Studies Centre at ISEAS from March 2008 to August 2015. He was also an adjunct professor at the Lee Kuan Yew School of Public Policy, National University of Singapore until 2015. During his time at ISEAS, he authored four books: *Southeast Asia in Search of an ASEAN Community* (2006), *ASEAN* (2008), *The ASEAN Regional Forum* (2009), and *Where in the World is the Philippines?* (2010). Severino was ASEAN secretary-general from 1998 to 2002 and served in various high-level capacities in the Department of Foreign Affairs of the Philippines including as the undersecretary of foreign affairs and ambassador to Malaysia. He twice served as the ASEAN senior official for the Philippines. Sadly, Severino passed away on 19 April 2019 while this book was going to press.

Siew Yean Tham is a senior fellow at ISEAS-Yusof Ishak Institute in Singapore and an adjunct professor at the Institute of Malaysian and International Studies (IKMAS), Universiti Kebangsaan Malaysia (UKM). She was formerly a director and professor at IKMAS, UKM. She has served as a consultant to national and international agencies, including the World Bank, ADB, and the Asian Development Bank Institute. Her research interests and publications are in foreign direct investment, international trade, trade policies, and industrial development in Malaysia and ASEAN. Her recent publications include *Moving Up the Value Chain in ICT: ASEAN Trade with China* (2016), *Institutionalizing East Asia* (for "Institutionalization of economic cooperation in East Asia" co-authored with Sueo Sudo, 2016), and the *Journal of Contemporary Asia* (with Andrew Jia Yi Kam and Nor Izzatina Aziz). She has a PhD in economics from the University of Rochester, US.

ABBREVIATIONS

ACIA	ASEAN Comprehensive Investment Agreement
AEC	ASEAN Economic Community
AFAS	ASEAN Framework Agreement on Services
AFC	Asian financial crisis
AFTA	ASEAN Free Trade Area
AIA	ASEAN Investment Area
AIC	ASEAN Industrial Complementation
AICO	ASEAN Industrial Cooperation
AIJV	ASEAN Industrial Joint Ventures
AIP	ASEAN Industrial Projects
AMS	ASEAN member state
APEC	Asia-Pacific Economic Cooperation
APTA	ASEAN Preferential Trading Arrangements
ASA	Association of Southeast Asia
ASEAN	Association of Southeast Asian Nations
CEPT	Common Effective Preferential Tariff
CLMV	Cambodia, Lao People's Democratic Republic, Myanmar, Viet Nam
EEC	European Economic Community
ETP	Economic Transformation Programme
EU	European Union
FDI	foreign direct investment
FTA	free trade agreement
GATS	General Agreement on Trade in Services
GATT	General Agreement on Tariffs and Trade
GDP	gross domestic product
GLC	government-linked company
IAI	Initiative for ASEAN Integration
ISEAS	Institute of Southeast Asian Studies
ISO	International Organization for Standardization
Lao PDR	Lao People's Democratic Republic
Maphilindo	Malaysia–Philippines–Indonesia
MERCOSUR	Mercado Común del Sur (Common Market of the South)

MFN	most favored nation
MNC	multinational corporation
NAFTA	North American Free Trade Agreement
NAM	Non-Aligned Movement
NEM	New Economic Model (Malaysia)
NEP	New Economic Policy (Malaysia)
NIE	newly industrialized economy
PRC	People's Republic of China
PTA	preferential trading arrangement
R&D	research and development
RCEP	Regional Comprehensive Economic Partnership Agreement
ROO	rule of origin
SMEs	small and medium-sized enterprises
TEL	temporary exclusion list
TPP	Trans-Pacific Partnership
TRIMS	Trade-Related Investment Measures
UN	United Nations
UNCTAD	United Nations Conference on Trade and Development
US	United States
WTO	World Trade Organization
ZOPFAN	Zone of Peace, Freedom and Neutrality

INTRODUCTORY REMARKS

Narongchai Akrasanee

Note: Narongchai Akrasanee, an early contributor to ASEAN and a pioneer of AFTA, delivered this during the High-Level Workshop on the Evolving Nature of ASEAN's Economic Cooperation: Original Vision and Current Practice held at the ISEAS–Yusof Ishak Institute in Singapore.

It could be said that my story of the Association of Southeast Asian Nations (ASEAN) has developed over the years from the two words: interest and opportunity. The "interest" began during my studies in Australia and the United States in the 1960s, when I wrote my dissertation on protectionism. The "opportunity" first arose when I came back to Thailand, my home country, and started working. I was determined to fight protectionism, which at that time was basically industrial policies.

In the early 1970s, when countries in the region like Malaysia and Singapore started opening their economies, I had opportunities to work with the National Economic and Social Development Board of Thailand. My work was on industrial and trade policies. And when the first ASEAN Summit was held in Bali in 1976, the agenda on economic cooperation—to which I had made some contribution—was very much derived from the recommendations of the Kansu report. The recommendations were also the origin of the ASEAN Preferential Trading Arrangements (APTA) and the ASEAN Industrial Projects (AIP).

Before economic cooperation was brought to discussion in 1976–1977, political and security issues dominated the ASEAN agenda. The economic issue was brought up at the first summit, and became ASEAN's major concern during and after the second oil crisis in 1979. The ASEAN Task Force to work on ASEAN cooperation issues was established in 1985.

I recall Thailand's active involvement in the ASEAN Task Force in 1985–1986, which produced a comprehensive report on ASEAN cooperation.

As history allowed, ASEAN had an opportunity in 1989–1990 to work with Cambodia, the Lao People's Democratic Republic (Lao PDR), Myanmar, and Viet Nam (CLMV), whose market economy strategies had started to produce results. This period saw great assistance from the Asian Development Bank through Greater Mekong Subregion projects in the CLMV countries. This was also the time when ASEAN started its expansion, building on the strong debate over Myanmar's membership.

Negotiations on the ASEAN Free Trade Area (AFTA) started in September 1991 and concluded in January 1992 with the signing of the AFTA Agreement in Singapore in February of that year. Most of the countries were very willing to conduct the negotiations. The negotiations therefore went very smoothly and were finalized quickly.

Having worked for the Government of Thailand since 1974, I became deeply involved in ASEAN issues. When I was the minister of commerce in 1996–1997, I had opportunities to work with other economic ministers to deepen ASEAN cooperation in the economic sector. The ASEAN Economic Ministers' Meeting in Cebu in 1997 laid the foundation for the Cebu Declaration on the Blueprint of the ASEAN Charter in 2007, followed by the ASEAN Charter, which came into effect in 2008.

Even as it focuses on the common goal of regional cooperation, ASEAN continues to work with regional and global external partners, as its principle is open regionalism. One of the most important turning points in ASEAN cooperation with external partners was its participation in the Asia-Pacific Economic Cooperation (APEC) Economic Leaders' Meeting in the United States in 1993. Examples of ASEAN cooperation initiatives include the ASEAN Plus Three (ASEAN plus Japan, the People's Republic of China, and the Republic of Korea), the East Asia Summit, and the ASEAN Plus Six (the Plus Three countries, Australia, India, and New Zealand). The agreements between ASEAN and its partners have helped reinforce the so-called "open economy" of Asian countries.

As for Thailand, moving forward beyond 2015, ASEAN has become "central" to the country's development strategy. In terms of economic cooperation, the Strategy for Future Development of Thailand outlines three layers: (i) the first layer—which is the closest one to Thailand and which involves the CLMV countries—highlights the significance of the regional production and market base; (ii) the second layer relates to the ASEAN mainland and ASEAN maritime areas for an optimal allocation of resources under the ASEAN Economic Community 2015, which requires

Thailand's appropriate policies to work on its most competitive areas; (iii) the third relates to the "ASEAN Plus" mechanism and suggests the internationalization of Thailand's economic policies to function within different mechanisms.

I shared with you how I was involved in ASEAN and how the idea of ASEAN economic cooperation developed. As for Thailand's policy strategy concerning ASEAN, I am very optimistic this is the way for countries like Thailand—a developing country in Southeast Asia, surrounded by the fast-growing CLMV countries and open economies like Malaysia, Singapore, and Indonesia as a big neighbor—to have better access to each other and to work together for regional development and prosperity.

The beginnings of regional cooperation. Indonesia signed the ASEAN Declaration with Malaysia, the Philippines, Singapore, and Thailand in 1967 (photo from the ASEAN Secretariat Photo Archives).

CHAPTER 1

THE EVOLUTION OF ASEAN: AN OVERVIEW

Jayant Menon and Cassey Lee

Introduction

The Association of Southeast Asian Nations (ASEAN) was formally established in August 1967.[1] In a region regaining independence and plagued by conflict since the end of the Second World War, ASEAN strived, first and foremost, to forge diplomatic cohesion among its members. Its five original members—Indonesia, Malaysia, the Philippines, Singapore, and Thailand—signed the broadly defined Bangkok Declaration. In general, its objectives were "To accelerate the economic growth, social progress and cultural development in the region.... To promote regional peace and stability.... To promote active collaboration and mutual assistance... in the economic, social, cultural, technical, and administrative spheres." Subsequently, ASEAN grew into today's close-knit group—holding some 700 meetings a year on economic, political, cultural, educational, and security issues. One of ASEAN's greatest achievements has been to effectively promote itself regionally and internationally through a wide range of initiatives.

Hill and Menon (2014) distinguish four more or less distinct phases in ASEAN's evolution. ASEAN was born in 1967 partly out of the highly uncertain regional and global environment at the time—one overshadowed by conflict. Earlier attempts at establishing a regional association, such as the Association of Southeast Asia (ASA), and the "Malay"-based group Maphilindo (Malaysia–Philippines–Indonesia), were plagued by internecine disputes. ASEAN's first leaders—several newly installed—therefore focused primarily on building regional harmony.

The second phase began with the Bali Summit in February 1976. This first meeting of ASEAN leaders marked the start of formal regional cooperation initiatives. These included the Agreement on ASEAN Preferential Trading Arrangements (APTA), five ASEAN Industrial Projects (AIPs), the ASEAN

---

[1] The literature on ASEAN and its development is voluminous. In addition to Hill and Menon (2014), see Chia (2011), and the references cited in both these papers.

Industrial Complementation (AIC) program, and ASEAN Industrial Joint Ventures (AIJV). The APTA was the most significant—the first attempt to promote intra-ASEAN trade through institutional integration and regional trade preferences. The AIPs, on the other hand, aimed to establish large-scale, intergovernmental projects in each ASEAN member state. The AIC and AIJV were to specialize in complementary products and facilitate pooling of resources. However, none of these four economic cooperation programs had any significant impact on regional economic relations. Indeed, they were explicitly designed for minimal effect, reflecting members' unwillingness—and inability at the time—to pursue either trade liberalization or regional integration. There was little further progress during the 1980s.

A third phase started in 1992 with a Leaders' Summit announcing the ASEAN Free Trade Area (AFTA). This was a clear break with the past. The emphasis was on stronger economic cooperation and, for the first time, "free trade" became the regional objective. There was a clear implementation timetable, employing a "negative list" approach—all goods trade was to be covered under AFTA unless explicitly excluded.

ASEAN leaders built on this renewed vigor by extending its geographic spread and commercial depth. Brunei Darussalam had joined in 1984. But ASEAN turned a historic corner in 1995 as Viet Nam was welcomed, followed by the Lao People's Democratic Republic (Lao PDR) and Myanmar in 1997, and finally Cambodia in 1999. The addition of these so-called CLMV countries brought ASEAN to its current 10-country membership.

Having grown in strength and number—and its ambitious program of economic and trade reforms—ASEAN stood out to the developing world as a successful example of regional cooperation and integration worthy of emulation. ASEAN was the most resilient regional group among countries of the developing world. However, just as the original leaders' dream of "one Southeast Asia" began to fall in place, the 1997 Asian financial crisis struck.

For the ASEAN region, the crisis had two principal effects. First, it lost some of its commercial attractiveness—the People's Republic of China (PRC) and India were largely unaffected by the crisis. Moreover, as an institution, ASEAN was seen by many as ineffective and feeble, unable to respond decisively in time of crisis. The second effect was more positive. The Asian financial crisis led to a general rethinking toward deepening regional economic cooperation—the need to develop the capacity for some sort of coordinated macroeconomic response to avert future crises.

This led to the fourth phase of ASEAN's evolution, defined by two key features: one being the rapid return to economic growth; the second being the struggle to better articulate its rationale and identity against the backdrop of a fast-changing regional and global environment. This led to a plethora of initiatives affecting commercial policy architecture.

These features shaped the region's commercial policy this century in four ways—all posing new and difficult challenges. The first is the spread of free trade agreements (FTAs). Singapore in particular, frustrated with ASEAN's slow progress, broke ranks through a bold strategy of signing FTAs with its global trade partners. While it initially caused strain within the grouping, it ultimately had a domino effect, as other ASEAN member states felt compelled to follow suit. As the FTA phenomenon expanded to third-party agreements with important trading partners, ASEAN members had to join to preserve market access and retain their market share with traditional trading partners. This domino effect came from multiple sources and was self-reinforcing, ensuring the proliferation of FTAs over a relatively short time.

Second, it became clear that ASEAN was too small to address many of the broader, postcrisis issues associated with macroeconomic coordination. To help organize future crisis response and prevention—including the building of regional financial safety nets—the large international reserves accumulated by the PRC, Japan, and the Republic of Korea (itself a crisis-affected country) dictated that these economies would need to be major players in any broader regional and international agreement.

Third, today ASEAN has largely completed the "easy phase" of intraregional trade liberalization. Import duties for 99.20% of committed tariff lines were eliminated by the ASEAN-6 and 90.85% by the CLMV. On average, ASEAN members have 96% of their tariff lines at 0%, and this was expected to reach 98.67% by 2018 (ASEAN 2016). What remains are politically more sensitive tariff lines, such as heavy industry and food crops—iron (steel) and rice in many countries, and some "sacred cows" such as automobiles in Malaysia.

Fourth, the rise of production networks or supply chains of intermediate goods (and services) questions the viability of any FTA that does not multilateralize concessions. East Asia and ASEAN have dominated this fast-growing segment of international trade. Clearly, the management of global production facilities, sourcing inputs from many countries for assembly in a single location, is fundamentally incompatible with the proliferation of FTAs. Most countries have multiple FTAs, each with specific—and rarely compatible—rules of origin.

ASEAN has significant achievements to its credit. First, it remains an effective functioning entity—far stronger than many other regional organizations in the developing world. Second, for a region characterized by great diversity and past political conflict, Southeast Asia has been largely peaceful since the mid-1980s, as the CLMV states progressively reentered the regional and international mainstream. Nonetheless, while border skirmishes persist, most conflicts have been internal. As recent maritime territorial claims in the region have shown, economic progress on cooperation cannot be divorced from the geopolitical challenges facing ASEAN as a whole. Indeed, these events remind us that ASEAN was born as a politico-security pact, with the economic agenda a more recent experiment. Given the interdependence between economics and geopolitics, however, ASEAN as an institution will have to confront and resolve these challenges if it is to maximize progress on its joint economic potential.

ASEAN's third and most important achievement has been, in aggregate, its rapid economic development and rising living standards. One can debate how much ASEAN as an institution has helped. But it is undeniable that the region's leaders' determination to forge more harmonious relations has helped facilitate this rapid economic development. In particular, the engagement with post-conflict Viet Nam, the Lao PDR, and Cambodia during their early stage of economic liberalization, after decades of acrimony and one of the most destructive wars in recent memory, has been a signal achievement.

It is against this backdrop—and ASEAN's emerging challenges—that motivated this volume. With ASEAN past its 50th year, how should it position itself to face the challenges of the next half century and beyond? What can it do now to ensure its resilience is preserved and strengthened? Many of the contributors to this volume were pivotal in shaping ASEAN's original course—in conceptualizing its role, in designing its vision, and in promoting its utility. They share their insights by narrating their individual historical experiences, influenced to varying degrees by their home country perspectives, and using these to draw lessons to confront the challenges of the future.

This volume contains seven key chapters, as well as the introductory remarks by Narongchai Akrasanee, an important motivation behind this project and a key contributor to the discussions that went into shaping the original design and evolution of ASEAN. Key points in each of the seven chapters are summarized below.

Chapter 2 by Emil Salim: A country perspective of the early history of ASEAN necessitates a narrative of both domestic and external factors that influenced the formation of ASEAN. Salim begins his essay with a reflection on Sukarno's leadership from 1945 until the mid-1960s. This early period was marked by Sukarno's consolidation of political power domestically via the support of the military and communist party. Under his leadership, Indonesia moved away from Western colonial powers and aligned itself with other former colonized countries to form the Non-Alignment Movement. It was also a period of conflict with its former colonial master (the Netherlands) and neighboring countries (Malaysia).

A key turning point in Indonesian history was the downfall of Sukarno in 1967. The government under the new president, Suharto, faced considerable challenges, including concerns about the growing influence of communism in the region and massive domestic debt. These constitute the context of Indonesia's participation in the formation of ASEAN in 1967 which is based on the perceived need to establish a zone of peace and cooperation. Thus, Salim is of the view that the factors underlying the formation of ASEAN were politics and security even though these were not mentioned in the ASEAN Declaration.

As a result, ASEAN in its early years was perceived as a rather "loose" organization with little tangible progress. It took some time for the organization to consolidate cooperation and cohesiveness among its member states. Salim also notes that in the early days of ASEAN, formal and often informal interactions between ASEAN leaders were crucial for building trust among the country leaders.

Over the years since its formation, ASEAN has become a stronger organization in terms of cooperation in economic, political-security, and sociocultural matters. A more recent challenge that ASEAN faces is the development gap between the early members and the CLMV countries. However, he notes that this development gap has been reduced in recent years due to the rapid growth of the CLMV countries. ASEAN continues to focus on economic convergence among its members. As Salim notes, one objective of the ASEAN Economic Community is to close these gaps through economies of scale and efficiency in production network processes. An important task toward achieving this goal is to persuade ASEAN citizens, including Indonesians, that they will benefit from greater regional integration.

Salim also opines that Indonesia, as the largest country in ASEAN, plays an important role in ASEAN. It has played the role of mediator in situations of conflict among other ASEAN member states. Indonesia's domestic political change following the fall of Suharto has influenced the country's role in ASEAN. For example, the political transformation in the post-Suharto period has led Indonesia to urge ASEAN to focus more on governance, human rights, democracy, and sustainable development—issues highlighted in the ASEAN Charter. Despite some initial disagreements on the inclusion of political and security issues, the ASEAN Charter was eventually promulgated, marking a new step toward a legal entity with a more formalized structure of regional governance.

Salim highlights five major developments in the relationships between ASEAN and non-ASEAN countries as well as within ASEAN:

(i)   There is stronger competition for resources to meet the domestic demand of ASEAN members and their neighboring countries.

(ii) The rise of a stronger and assertive PRC has raised concerns of not only its neighboring countries but also major advanced countries.

(iii) ASEAN is currently seen as putting too much emphasis on economic cooperation while almost neglecting its political-security and sociocultural aspects.

(iv) ASEAN members are experiencing a "trust deficit" with a lack of trust among member states.

(v)   As global demand has weakened recently due to growth slowdown in advanced countries, ASEAN has become more relevant as a source of global growth.

Leadership in the current ASEAN is a major issue. In this regard, Salim observes that some members have resisted Indonesia's leadership on many occasions. To overcome this problem, Salim suggests that Indonesia needs to assure other ASEAN member states that it speaks and acts for the good of all ASEAN.

Looking ahead, Salim emphasizes the need to build greater trust among ASEAN member states. They should also strengthen economic cooperation to help achieve productivity-led sustainable development.

Chapter 3 by Delia Albert: In her essay, Albert describes the Southeast Asian region in the early years after the Second World War as one that was marked by bilateral territorial disputes and the common external threat from the spread of communism. Security was thus a major factor that motivated the founding members of ASEAN to engage with neighboring countries and seek ways of resolving disputes and achieve peace and stability in the region.

A number of precursor organizations to ASEAN were important in planting the seed of regional cooperation—ASA and Maphilindo. ASA, in particular, was an important predecessor institution. This was highlighted in the remarks by Narciso Ramos, then the Philippine Secretary of Foreign Affairs.

A key aspect of regional cooperation to maintain peace and stability was the "ASEAN Way" of consultation and consensus. Consultations between ASEAN leaders (especially foreign ministers) were very important for resolving bilateral problems (such as territorial disputes) and for developing trust in the late 1960s and 1970s. Informal talks played a key role. Leaders during this period also began to engage more in bilateral visits and talks.

The idea for regional economic cooperation emerged at a later stage sometime around the early 1970s. The idea of an ASEAN free trade area was proposed in 1975 by the Philippines and Singapore. In this regard, a key turning point was the United Nations (UN) study on intra-ASEAN economic cooperation titled "Economic Cooperation among Member Countries of the Association of Southeast Asian Nations" and the UN agenda to establish the New International Economic Order. The UN report was also regarded as an important reference to address the stagnating economic growth in the region. Recommendations in the report included selected trade liberalization, joint implementation of new larger-scale projects, and a "Complementary Agreements System."

The proposal of the Philippines, with support from Singapore, for the establishment of an ASEAN free trade area as early as 1975 was watered down to that of a preferential trading agreement. In view of this development, the Philippines proposed an across-the-board tariff reduction of 10%–15%. This eventually led to the establishment of the ASEAN Free Trade Area (AFTA) in 1992.

External pressure was key to its establishment—"Fortress Europe" and the North American Free Trade Agreement. AFTA and other subsequent initiatives such as the ASEAN Framework Agreement on Services, ASEAN Investment Area, ASEAN Trade in Goods Agreement, and ASEAN Economic Community were driven by the fear of being left out in the global competition for preferential deals.

Albert also opines that the achievement of peace and stability of the region brought about a peace dividend in the form of economic dynamism in the region. The key challenge in the future, according to Albert, is to strengthen the connection across citizens of ASEAN member states in such a way as to enhance shared values.

Chapter 4 by Rodolfo C. Severino: An analysis of the origins and evolution of ASEAN is presented here. The context for the emergence of ASEAN in the 1960s was regional conflicts in the form of territorial disputes among Southeast Asian countries, the threat of communism (Cold War), and the involvement of the United States in the Viet Nam War.

During this period, Southeast Asian countries were keen to avoid the region becoming a locus of conflict between the superpowers. Related to this is the nonalignment stance that a number of countries in the region had taken.

The two original goals reflected these developments:

(i)   To prevent the historical disputes among its member states from developing into armed conflict.
(ii) To keep the major external powers from using the region as an arena for their quarrels.

Severino argues that these two goals remain relevant to ASEAN even though they were not fully reflected in the ASEAN Declaration. He notes that, of the seven "aims and purposes" in the ASEAN Declaration, only one dealt with "regional peace and stability." This, he opines, was because the objectives were essentially disguised by economic and cultural cooperation lest ASEAN member states be accused of forming a military alliance or defense pact.

Severino notes, however, that of late, ASEAN member states have found it difficult to maintain shared strategic interests, particularly in establishing a joint position on maritime territorial claims.

There is a strategic dimension to regional economic integration (and sociocultural and environmental cooperation), which reinforces politics and security. Though economic cooperation was not the main goal of ASEAN in its early years, it has become more important over the years. Economic cooperation was first recognized as a legitimate ASEAN endeavor in 1976.

Economic cooperation initially focused on preferential trading arrangements and industrial cooperation. The former entailed the removal of quantitative restrictions and other nontariff barriers within certain time frames. Despite the lowering of tariffs via preferential trading arrangements, nontariff barriers remain high. Industrial cooperation took the form of AIPs, in which each member state is given a regional monopoly on a certain manufactured product or group of products. This endeavor was not very successful due to countries changing their minds on the targeted projects as well as countries abandoning their projects. ASEAN members were also reluctant to see a reduction in their option to invest in industries that were similar to those allocated to another country.

Economic cooperation became more important in the 1990s. A number of factors provided impetus to ASEAN's economic cooperation. These include the rise of the PRC as a major foreign direct investment (FDI) destination and exporter. Rising FDI and establishment of production chains in ASEAN following the Plaza Accord was another factor. Global trading agreements also evolved with the establishment of MERCOSUR, the North American Free Trade Agreement, and the World Trade Organization (WTO). The AFTA Agreement was concluded at the Singapore ASEAN Summit in January 1992. The next landmark in ASEAN's economic cooperation was the ASEAN Economic Community, first proposed in 2002 and established in December 2015.

Chapter 5 by Suthad Setboonsarng and Chayut Setboonsarng: The evolution of economic cooperation in ASEAN and its governing institutions as well as the current progress with the AEC are highlighted in this chapter. The Setboonsarngs see global economic developments playing a huge role in driving economic cooperation and integration in ASEAN. They divide these developments into five major time periods, or "waves":

- The first wave covers the colonization period from 1870 to 1945, when ASEAN member states were mainly tapped as sources of raw materials by colonial masters.

- The second wave spans 1945–1975, the period of decolonization and nation-building, during which ASEAN member states began to build the foundations for economic growth in the region.
- The third wave from 1975 to 1992 covers the decades of impressive growth preceding the Asian financial crisis. This period was marked by increasing integration with both Asian and global markets, and the beginnings of regional production networks.
- The fourth wave from 1992 to 2006 covers the pre- and post-Asian financial crisis years, which were marked by an intensification in regional cooperation initiatives. Some of the landmark initiatives adopted during this period were AFTA, the ASEAN Comprehensive Investment Agreement, and the ASEAN Framework Agreement on Services. The decision to create an ASEAN Community was also made during this period.
- The fifth wave covers the years just prior to the 2008 global financial crisis, all the way up to the present. The authors qualify the global financial crisis as a "pivotal event" that caused a rebalancing in the global economy, with Asia at the center of future growth. ASEAN economic cooperation is currently focused on increasing engagement with external partners, as evidenced by initiatives such as the East Asia Summit and the Regional Comprehensive Economic Partnership (RCEP).

The Setboonsarngs then trace the evolution of governing bodies of ASEAN, highlighting the shift in its power base from foreign ministers to finance ministers, before focusing on key governance challenges. They note that ASEAN's broadening cooperation agenda has placed a considerable amount of strain on ASEAN's financial and human resources. They argue that work on regulatory issues could be delegated to the ASEAN Secretariat, but that it is already overstretched as it is. The ASEAN Secretariat's responsibilities have increased, but this has not been matched by an increase in its annual operating budget or salary scale. They also note that the flexibility that characterizes ASEAN cooperation and decision-making has enabled ASEAN member states to implement commitments in line with their levels of readiness. However, given the increasing complexity of ASEAN's cooperation areas, member states must become open to alternatives such as majority or supermajority decision-making.

Finally, they turn their attention to the AEC, first looking at progress before considering the remaining challenges. The authors argue that a single production base has already been realized in certain industries such as consumer electronics, electrical appliances, automotive, and textile and garments. This has strengthened ASEAN's role as a manufacturing hub and regional base of operations for multinational corporations seeking to support their business operations in Asia and the Pacific. Other notable achievements include ASEAN measures in trade facilitation, such as the ASEAN Single Window and mutual recognition standards, and ongoing harmonization of regulatory and industry standards.

These achievements notwithstanding, a number of challenges remain. The Setboonsarngs also highlight the following:

- Across the ASEAN member states, trade and investment barriers remain in certain sensitive sectors such as agriculture, aviation, and financial services.
- Although the ASEAN Dispute Settlement Mechanism has been in place for almost 2 decades, it remains unused. Disputes are still settled informally through negotiations, although at least one investor-state dispute has been settled under an ASEAN arbitration tribunal under the ASEAN Comprehensive Investment Agreement.
- Although ASEAN member states have become deeply embedded in global production networks, they capture only a small share of the retail value of the goods they help produce.
- Income disparity across the ASEAN member states is increasing and is expected to worsen by 2020. To address this, the authors urge ASEAN to prioritize financial inclusion and literacy, among a host of other related measures.

Chapter 6 by Chia Siow Yue: In this chapter, Chia examines Singapore's motivations for engaging with ASEAN and other partners, its position in relation to ASEAN's evolving economic agenda, and the areas for future cooperation.

She begins by tracing the evolution of Singapore's foreign and trade policy since the 1960s. She writes that Singapore's foreign policy has been motivated by the need to ensure Singapore's economic and political survival, given the country's size and limited resource endowments relative to its ASEAN neighbors. Consistent with its foreign policy, Singapore's trade policy has traditionally been outward-oriented and focused on creating an export-led and FDI-led economy. There are minimal restrictions on exports, imports, and FDI, with services trade becoming increasingly open. For Chia, this openness—coupled with sound macroeconomic governance and investments in infrastructure and human capital—has helped transform

Singapore "from a regional entrepôt into an export manufacturing platform and services hub, and further into a knowledge-based economy."

Among the ASEAN member states, Singapore currently has the most number of FTAs, which it uses as tools for both economic and foreign policy. Chia writes that, beyond the more traditional goals of securing market access and attracting FDI, Singapore uses FTAs to establish itself as a services hub and anchor production networks and multinational corporations based in the country. Singapore also uses FTAs to go beyond plurilateral and multilateral trade liberalization, particularly in light of protracted negotiations at the multilateral level. Singapore's bilateral FTAs are WTO-consistent (General Agreement on Tariffs and Trade Article XXIV) and WTO-plus (General Agreement on Trade in Services V), which minimizes their trade diversionary effects.

Chia observes that compared to other ASEAN member states, Singapore has traditionally been more willing to liberalize trade and investments, as evinced by its propensity for unilateral liberalization. This position has often been at odds with those of other ASEAN members. But in keeping with the ASEAN Way, Singapore has "[treaded] softly in line with the comfort zone of others," at times supporting ASEAN agreements despite having misgivings about their usefulness. This was true in the case of the ASEAN Preferential Trading Arrangements (APTA). While the APTA was ASEAN's first formal attempt at encouraging intra-ASEAN trade, Chia writes that it ultimately had very limited impact on trade liberalization. She ascribes this to a lack of serious intent and political will. She points out that a number of industrial cooperation schemes were also largely unsuccessful.

While these early attempts at economic integration fell short of their ambitions, Chia notes that by the 1990s, several domestic and external factors helped the ASEAN economic agenda transition from cooperation to integration. Singapore played an active role in pushing for integration initiatives. For example, Chia reports considerable progress in tariff reduction and/or elimination under AFTA, and achievements under the ASEAN Industrial Cooperation scheme in promoting production networks in the automobile and electronics industries. However, she also highlights slow progress in the removal of nontariff barriers, services liberalization under the ASEAN Framework Agreement on Services, and investment liberalization under the ASEAN Investment Area. Chia cites the results of the 2001 Midterm Review of the Ha Noi Plan of Action, which identified reasons for implementation delays, including (i) weak commitment to some of the decisions to promote liberalization and cooperation programs;

(ii) conflicting interests at the domestic level; (iii) legislative changes to ratify agreements and commitments; and (iv) lack of technical capacity and financial resources to support implementation.

Turning her attention to the AEC, Chia points out that even ASEAN's own AEC Scorecard has revealed serious shortfalls in implementation (although the data she cites cover only the 2008–2011 period). Remaining bottlenecks include addressing nontariff barriers; improving trade facilitation; liberalizing services and investment; promoting mobility of skilled labor by removing legal and regulatory restrictions to market entry; and improving awareness of the AEC's opportunities and challenges.

The remaining challenges notwithstanding, Chia remains optimistic about ASEAN regional integration. She stresses that major strides have been taken over the last 4 decades, and that ASEAN's brand of open regionalism has served the region well. Moving forward, she identifies issues that must be addressed beyond 2015, including narrowing the development gap in ASEAN and expanding economic integration through initiatives such as the RCEP.

Chapter 7 by Tham Siew Yean: This chapter contains a narrative of Malaysia's perspective on ASEAN economic cooperation. In the introductory section, she points out that Malaysia's reason for cofounding ASEAN was politically motivated—that is, to preserve peace and to balance the roles of outside powers. Though initially skeptical, the country's first prime minister was eventually persuaded by ministry officials and Thailand to join ASEAN.

Tham frames her discussion of the evolution of ASEAN economic cooperation in terms of three distinct phases:

The first is pre-AFTA period (1976–1983). This is a period which saw the attempts to implement the AIPs (1976), APTA (1977), AIC scheme (1981), and AIJV (1983). These attempts were not very successful due to the vested interest of the countries to protect their domestic markets. Tham also discussed the impact of the recession in the mid-1980s, which led to economic liberalization.

The second is the AFTA period. The discussions during this mostly focused on the conflict between AFTA and Malaysia's industrial policy of second-stage import substitution (heavy industries). The latter affected the country's reception toward the ASEAN Industrial Cooperation scheme

(1996) and the ASEAN Investment Area (1995). Similarly, Malaysia was lukewarm toward the ASEAN Framework Agreement on Services (1995) due to the inward orientation of its services sector.

The third is the post-AFTA period. In this period, during which the AEC was launched (2003), the Malaysian economy had slowed down and became less attractive as an FDI destination. This made the country more receptive to the establishment of the ASEAN Comprehensive Investment Agreement in 2009. Beyond this period, the rise of the PRC and the importance of Japan also prompted Malaysia to propose the formation of a regional trading group, which originally excluded the United States. Tham argues the idea of an East Asian regional grouping eventually took root as the ASEAN Plus Three process and the East Asia Summit.

In the last segment of her essay, Tham reflects on the future of ASEAN and Malaysia's economic policies. She notes that the new government elected in 2018 has begun reconsidering Malaysia's liberalization commitments and is veering toward the adoption of more protectionist policies. Given recent developments, she opines that "Malaysia is unlikely to press for a more rules-based ASEAN," and instead "continue to support flexibility in liberalization commitments as well as in the implementation of ASEAN's commitments."

Chapter 8 by Florian A. Alburo: The evolution of ASEAN's economic agenda and the Philippines' readiness for the AEC is explored in this chapter. Alburo begins with a brief analysis of how ASEAN's economic agenda has evolved since its establishment. Like the other authors in this volume, Alburo notes an improvement in both the process and scope of this agenda. In its nascent stages, ASEAN's economic cooperation agreements were essentially "country-centered" and driven by bureaucrats, with coverage that was often fragmented and highly selective with respect to the products or sectors to be liberalized. In the 1990s, however, the pace of initiatives accelerated, and their focus, content, and technical nature improved. Alburo highlights the "increasing sophistication of the agreements beginning in 2001, with more focus on their regional aspects or their implications on intra-regional trade." He gives credit to the ASEAN Secretariat for its role in improving the content of ASEAN's agreements.

Alburo briefly draws parallels between the establishment of the European Economic Community (EEC) and ASEAN's economic agenda. He observes that while there are similarities in the original motivations for the European Community and ASEAN (both were intended to bring peace and stability to their respective regions), the EEC and the AEC are more different than the same: their end goals are different, as are their institutional mechanisms and the binding nature of their agreements. Their starting conditions are also different, inasmuch as ASEAN member states exhibit more diversity than EEC members. At the same time, the euro crisis since 2009 has revealed the EEC's vulnerability, making it less of the standard for integration than it once was.

The attention is then turned to the Philippines' readiness for the AEC, particularly the first pillar (single market and production base). Alburo's analysis reveals the following:

- Fears that the AEC will flood the country with intra-ASEAN imports seem unfounded. ASEAN's share of Philippine imports never breached 20% between 1993 and 2012, and this is unlikely to change given that the country's most favored nation and Common Effective Preferential Tariff (CEPT) rates have fallen simultaneously. The Philippines' adherence to the CEPT time line and efforts to improve competitiveness in products under the exclusion list also suggest that the Philippines is ready for the AEC as far as imports are concerned.
- However, with regard to exports, the Philippines lags behind other ASEAN member states in quality benchmarks. Quality-driven product differentiation for Philippine exports will be critical, particularly for those that have attained some maturity.
- There has been uneven progress and readiness in the other elements of the first AEC pillar. In services liberalization, the Philippines' commitments under the AEC hardly differ from its commitments under the General Agreement on Trade in Services. The country has also been slow to ratify regional agreements on transport services liberalization, despite the potential gains from opening up this sector. In capital and investment liberalization, readiness will depend more on domestic reforms than regional agreements. As for liberalizing skilled labor flows, mutual recognition agreements must be complemented by efforts to improve market access for skilled labor.

Other AEC pillars are discussed briefly, as Alburo observes that commitments under the first pillar form the core of the AEC. On the second pillar (competitive economic region), he notes that the Philippines has promulgated a new law creating the Office for Competition in the Department of Justice as the designated competition body. He also sees progress in consumer protection, intellectual property rights, infrastructure development, taxation, and e-commerce. On the third pillar (equitable economic development), he acknowledges regional initiatives on development of small and medium-sized enterprises and the Initiative for ASEAN Integration, but stresses the importance of national-level interventions in addressing the development divide. On the fourth pillar (integration into the global economy), he opines that measuring progress based on the entry of force of FTAs is insufficient; the content and welfare effects of these FTAs must also be considered.

Alburo concludes by stressing that the Philippines' readiness for the AEC ultimately hinges on the country's readiness for wider global integration. He emphasizes that this is true for the other ASEAN member states as well, and correctly characterizes readiness for the AEC as a "by-product of global readiness." Viewed in this light, Alburo notes that the Philippines still has some distance to go before it becomes fully ready for global integration.

References

Association of Southeast Asian Nations (ASEAN). 2016. Joint Media Statement, The 48th ASEAN Economic Ministers' Meeting. 3 August, Vientiane, Lao People's Democratic Republic.

Chia, S.Y. 2011. Association of Southeast Asian Nations Economic Integration: Developments and Challenges. *Asian Economic Policy Review* 6(1): 43–63.

Hill, H. and J. Menon. 2014. ASEAN Economic Integration: Driven by Markets, Bureaucrats, or Both?" In M.E. Kreinin and M.G. Plummer, eds. *The Oxford Handbook of International Commercial Policy.* Oxford, UK: Oxford University Press.

Establishing regional diplomatic cohesion. The first summit of the Association of Southeast Asian Nations (ASEAN) was held in Bali, Indonesia, in 1976; ASEAN Leaders endorsed the Treaty of Amity and Cooperation in Southeast Asia and adopted the Bali Concord I (photos from the ASEAN Secretariat Photo Archives).

CHAPTER 2
ASEAN ECONOMIC COOPERATION: VISION, PRACTICE, AND CHALLENGES

Emil Salim

This chapter examines the domestic and external factors that have influenced ASEAN's evolution and traces the progression of Indonesia's participation in ASEAN. It also discusses the impact of the Plus Three countries on ASEAN's dynamic, and highlights the continuing importance of building trust and preserving peace in the region.

Introduction

The Association of Southeast Asian Nations (ASEAN) was founded in 1967 amid numerous uncertainties in the Southeast Asian region. Early members of ASEAN (Indonesia, the Philippines, Singapore, and Thailand) faced regional conflicts with each other or with other countries as open war had erupted in the region.

2.1   Indonesia in ASEAN: Past

Following Indonesia's independence in 1945, Sukarno, Indonesia's first president, was faced with challenges of building a nation that had been occupied for 350 years by the Dutch and for 3.5 years by the Japanese. He was widely known as a nation builder who created the nation on the basis of five fundamental principles, collectively known as the Pancasila: (i) believe in the one supreme God, (ii) justice and civilized humanity, (iii) the unity of Indonesia, (iv) democracy guided by the wisdom of people, and (v) social justice for all.

From the early to mid-1960s, Indonesia experienced dynamic domestic and foreign political activity. Sukarno secured his domestic authority with the support of the military forces, the Communist Party of Indonesia, and the parliament (of which half the members were appointed by him). At the time, he did not want to be associated with the West since he saw many of them as former colonialists. To elevate former colonized countries' bargaining power, President Sukarno, together with President Gamal Abdel Nasser of Egypt, Prime Minister Pandit Jawaharlal Nehru of India, President Josip Broz Tito of the former Yugoslavia, and President Kwame Nkrumah of Ghana formed the Non-Alignment Movement (NAM) based on the Asian–African Conference in Bandung in 1955. His basic obsession was to build the world anew, in which the Western forces need to be balanced by the new emerging nations.

During this period, Indonesia had conflicts with the Netherlands over West Irian and with Malaysia over the disputed border in Borneo or Kalimantan island. The latter conflict is known as "the Indonesia–Malaysia Confrontation." In the mid-1960s, Sukarno began to complement the NAM with new alliances with the People's Republic of China (PRC), Cambodia, the Democratic People's Republic of Korea, and North Viet Nam resulting in the formation of the "Beijing–Pyongyang–Ha Noi–Phnom Penh–Jakarta Axis."

However, with the downfall of Sukarno, following the alleged coup d'état by the Communist Party of Indonesia, things changed dramatically after Suharto succeeded Sukarno as president in 1967. Suharto had to face not only domestic political and economic turmoil inherited from the previous government, but also growing concerns about communist influence in the Southeast Asian region. Domestically, Indonesia inherited massive foreign debt from the previous government and needed money to pay for this debt. Suharto followed a more pragmatic approach in dealing with the domestic economic burden by accepting help from countries in the West to settle Indonesia's debt. Externally, Indonesia faced the same growing threat of communism as Viet Nam, which won the war with the United States (US). Communism had become a common threat to the countries in the Southeast Asian region.

As Sukarno had done in his earlier years, along the spirit of the 1945 Constitution of the Republic of Indonesia (Undang-Undang Dasara, or UUD 1945), Suharto developed "non-alignment" or "free and active" foreign policy, which emphasized neutrality ("free") and the need to proactively engage in a continuous effort to keeping peace within the region ("active"). Based on the need to establish a zone of peace and cooperation, Indonesia signed the ASEAN Declaration with Malaysia, the Philippines, Singapore, and Thailand in 1967, showing the group's commitment to meet the need for regional cooperation against a common enemy—the communist threat.

In 1967, ASEAN was merely a declaration, which was nonbinding. ASEAN's objectives were to accelerate economic growth, social progress, and cultural development; to promote peace and stability; to collaborate in agriculture and industry; and to expand trade. However, the key concerns— political stability and security in the region—were not explicitly mentioned in the ASEAN Declaration. As a result, ASEAN was often seen as a "loose" organization, and there was little tangible progress in the early years. ASEAN member states were fully aware that they formed this institution more for political objectives, stability, and security. It took some time for ASEAN to actually consolidate its cooperation and cohesiveness. Due most likely to Indonesia's population and land size, several ASEAN leaders—notably Lee Kuan Yew and Mahathir Mohamad—recognized on many occasions and at different periods that Suharto played a pivotal role in the success of ASEAN.

During its early years, ASEAN ministers and officials developed a good working relationship by building trust through regular and frequent meetings, officially and unofficially. ASEAN leaders played golf or had karaoke sessions together. It is usually during such a relaxed atmosphere that they exchanged ideas and informed each other of their domestic policies that fit into the ASEAN framework. Over time, this personal and relaxed ambience of meetings was helpful in building trust among ASEAN leaders. In every major situation, ASEAN sought consensus, avoided meddling in other members' sovereignty, and in the long run this cycle of trust built stronger bonds among member state leaders.

2.2   Indonesia in ASEAN: Present

After almost 50 years since ASEAN was born, the institution has experienced a major transformation from a merely "loose" to a stronger organization in cooperation in economic, political-security, and sociocultural matters. Nonetheless, development gaps between and within member states remain, and new substantial issues have emerged, particularly between early members and Cambodia, the Lao People's Democratic Republic (Lao PDR), Myanmar, and Viet Nam (collectively CLMV). Due to the different past colonial history and differences in legal, political, and governance systems among ASEAN member states, the key development indicators indicate that there are important cross-country differences. Table 2.1 shows several development statistics for ASEAN members. It clearly shows large development gaps among member states.

Table 2.1: ASEAN Key Development Statistics, 2017

AMS	Brunei Darussalam	Cambodia	Indonesia	Lao PDR	Malaysia	Myanmar	Philippines	Singapore	Thailand	Viet Nam
Access to electricity, rural (% of rural population)[a]	100.0	36.5	94.8	80.3	100.0	39.8	86.3	..	100.0	100.0
GDP growth (annual %)	1.3	6.8	5.1	6.9	5.9	6.4	6.7	3.6	3.9	6.8
GDP per capita (constant 2010 $)	31,439.90	1,135.20	4,130.70	1,730.40	11,521.50	1,484.20	2,891.40	55,235.50	6,125.70	1,834.70
High-technology exports (% of manufactured exports)[b]	17.9	0.4	5.8	33.6	43.0	7.6	55.1	48.9	21.5	26.9
Military expenditure (% of GDP)[c]	2.9	2.1	0.8	0.2	1.1	2.5	1.4	3.2	1.4	2.3
School enrollment, tertiary (% gross)[d]	30.9	13.1	27.9	17.2	44.1	16.0	35.3	..	45.9	28.3
Unemployment, total (% of total labor force) (modeled ILO estimate)	7.1	0.2	4.3	0.7	3.4	0.8	2.8	2.0	1.1	2.1

.. = not available, AMS = ASEAN member state, ASEAN = Association of Southeast Asian Nations, GDP = gross domestic product, Lao PDR = Lao People's Democratic Republic.

Notes:
[a] Data for 2016.
[b] Brunei Darussalam data for 2015; Viet Nam data for 2014.
[c] Lao PDR data for 2013.
[d] Cambodia and Thailand data for 2015; Brunei Darussalam, Indonesia, Lao PDR, Malaysia, and Viet Nam data for 2016.

Source: World Bank. World Development Indicators. https://databank.worldbank.org/data/reports.aspx?source=world-development-indicators (accessed 7 August 2018).

Singapore has the highest gross domestic product (GDP) per capita ($55,235.50) whereas Cambodia has the lowest ($1,135.20). The majority of the countries have a relatively low unemployment rate.

Despite the large development gaps in the region, the CLMV countries are moving toward convergence, and the development gaps between them and more advanced countries are rapidly declining. Their economies have grown much faster than non-CLMV countries in ASEAN, as shown in Table 2.2.

One objective of the ASEAN Economic Community (AEC) is to close the gaps between the ASEAN-6 and the CLMV countries through economies of scale and efficiency in production network processes. ASEAN is now seen and proven to be on its way to becoming an effective single market and production base.

During the 5 decades of ASEAN existence, it has proven to be a major economic growth center. It is estimated that ASEAN can become the fourth largest economy by 2050 with a population of 600 million people.

However, the main challenge is to convince ASEAN members to move further up to reap the benefits of this economic integration. For example, many people in Indonesia believe that Indonesia would be worse off from this integration due to its low product competitiveness, low productivity, and limited number of skilled workers. There is a growing concern that Indonesia could only sit and watch as other ASEAN member states' products and skilled labor flock to Indonesia's enormous market, which has a population of around 250 million and a growing middle class.

Indonesia looks upon Southeast Asia and Asia as a whole as a "dynamic equilibrium" in which ASEAN members would like political relations in the region to be integrative, cooperative, and peaceful. ASEAN has often relied on Indonesia for leadership due to its size, vibrant democracy, economic performance, and relative military strength. In the past, Indonesia has played an important and active role in ASEAN as a manager of crises, mediator of disputes, and creator of ideas, contributing to the transformation of the organization. For instance, Indonesia managed to persuade the Myanmar junta to permit foreign aid organizations into the country following the occurrence of Cyclone Nargis in 2008. Other examples include Indonesia's involvement in active diplomacy over the conflict between Thailand and Cambodia over the Preah Vihear Temple in 2011 and over the maritime territorial claims in the region (Roberts and Widyaningsih 2015).

Table 2.2: ASEAN Gross Domestic Product Growth Rates, 2000–2017

AMS	2000	2001	2002	2003	2004	2005	2006	2007	2008	2009	2010
Myanmar	13.7	11.3	12.0	13.8	13.6	13.6	13.1	12.0	10.3	10.6	9.6
Cambodia	10.7	7.4	6.6	8.5	10.3	13.3	10.8	10.2	6.7	0.1	6.0
Lao PDR	5.8	5.8	5.9	6.1	6.4	7.1	8.6	7.6	7.8	7.5	8.5
Viet Nam	6.8	6.2	6.3	6.9	7.5	7.5	7.0	7.1	5.7	5.4	6.4
Singapore	8.9	-1.0	4.2	4.4	9.5	7.5	8.9	9.1	1.8	-0.6	15.2
Philippines	4.4	2.9	3.6	5.0	6.7	4.8	5.2	6.6	4.2	1.1	7.6
Indonesia	4.9	3.6	4.5	4.8	5.0	5.7	5.5	6.3	6.0	4.6	6.2
Malaysia	8.9	0.5	5.4	5.8	6.8	5.3	5.6	6.3	4.8	-1.5	7.4
Thailand	4.5	3.4	6.1	7.2	6.3	4.2	5.0	5.4	1.7	-0.7	7.5
Brunei Darussalam	2.8	2.7	3.9	2.9	0.5	0.4	4.4	0.2	-1.9	-1.8	2.6

AMS	2011	2012	2013	2014	2015	2016	2017	Average
Myanmar	5.6	7.3	8.4	8.0	7.0	5.9	6.4	10.1
Cambodia	7.1	7.3	7.4	7.1	7.0	7.0	6.8	7.8
Lao PDR	8.0	8.0	8.0	7.6	7.3	7.0	6.9	7.2
Viet Nam	6.2	5.2	5.4	6.0	6.7	6.2	6.8	6.4
Singapore	6.4	4.1	5.1	3.9	2.2	2.4	3.6	5.3
Philippines	3.7	6.7	7.1	6.1	6.1	6.9	6.7	5.3
Indonesia	6.2	6.0	5.6	5.0	4.9	5.0	5.1	5.3
Malaysia	5.3	5.5	4.7	6.0	5.0	4.2	5.9	5.1
Thailand	0.8	7.2	2.7	1.0	3.0	3.3	3.9	4.0
Brunei Darussalam	3.7	0.9	-2.1	-2.3	-0.6	-2.5	1.3	0.8

AMS = ASEAN member state, ASEAN = Association of Southeast Asian Nations, GDP = gross domestic product, Lao PDR = Lao People's Democratic Republic.

Source: World Bank. World Development Indicators. https://databank.worldbank.org/data/reports.aspx?source=world-development-indicators (accessed 7 August 2018).

Moreover, Indonesia has created and proposed new innovative ideas that shape ASEAN's norms and institutions since the establishment of ASEAN. In a meeting in Bali in 2003, Singapore along with Indonesia proposed the formation of the AEC to strengthen economic cooperation. At the time, the Asian financial crisis had considerable negative impacts on ASEAN economies and greater regional integration was urgently needed to accelerate recovery.

Meanwhile, Indonesia experienced a significant political change from an authoritarian to a democratic regime. The movement is widely known as "Reformasi" or reformation. Indonesia tried to mirror this domestic spirit of reformation and shared its experiences with ASEAN by proposing that the group should not emphasize economic aspects only. Instead, it should also consider values such as good governance, human rights, democracy, and sustainable development. Before the meeting in Bali, the Government of Indonesia drafted policy document titled "Towards an ASEAN Security Community."

However, in 2003, there was some resistance to the inclusion of political and security issues such as human rights and democracy in the ASEAN Charter. This was due to differences in political systems within ASEAN (i.e., democratic vs. authoritarian regimes). As a result, political and security inclusiveness were delayed until a meeting in 2007, at which the ASEAN Charter was promulgated. The ASEAN Charter marked a great transformation from being merely a "loose" organization to a legal entity with a more formalized structure of regional governance. It also reaffirmed ASEAN's main principles of noninterference and consensus-based decision-making.

In recent years, there have been major developments in the relationships between ASEAN and non-ASEAN countries as well as within ASEAN.

First, there is stronger competition for resources to meet the domestic demand of ASEAN members and their neighboring countries. Initially, ASEAN was founded to curb ideological influences in the region. Now, however, ASEAN and countries around the East Asian region have to compete for resources. This has changed the power politics in the region. The PRC's claims over some areas are largely due to the country's efforts to secure resources for energy and food. The PRC's large population, rising middle class, rapid urbanization, and the end of its demographic bonus are several factors that have increased its demand for energy and food.

Second, the rise of a stronger and assertive PRC has raised concerns in not only its neighboring countries but also major advanced countries. ASEAN members tend to align themselves with one or more dominant countries such as the PRC, the US, and Japan. This current development reminds us of the regional conflicts before ASEAN was born. Stronger leadership is highly needed to unite ASEAN and avoid being dominated by more powerful countries.

Third, some countries see ASEAN as putting too much emphasis on economic cooperation while almost neglecting its political-security and sociocultural aspects. ASEAN started as a "loose" organization to unite its members against a common enemy, but has evolved into an "economic entity" with less emphasis on the other two aspects. Recent studies have shown that development that overemphasizes economic aspects will lead to worsening inequality, which disturbs social cohesiveness within a country and region. ASEAN has made significant progress in regional economic cooperation, but it has made little progress on developing the political-security and sociocultural communities. This indicates an imbalance between the three pillars of the ASEAN Community. One reason may be that economic development is easier to measure, whereas political-security and sociocultural issues can only be felt when a negative situation emerges. In 2012, the ASEAN summit could not produce a consensus. This showed that the sociopolitical aspects have fallen short at the expense of economic development in ASEAN. It also weakens the bargaining power of ASEAN.

Regional order is a necessary condition for the success of economic integration. Therefore, a proper balance between these three aspects should always be encouraged. Furthermore, the challenges of implementing ASEAN's three-pillar objectives are evident within the ASEAN member states, especially in economic integration. This is due to a lack of clear information on the benefits of economic integration, lack of trust, fear of the loss of regulatory control, and the power of domestic interests.

Fourth, ASEAN is currently experiencing a "trust deficit," where there is a lack of trust among member states. Less emphasis on the development of sociocultural aspects may have contributed to this lack of trust. In a high-level survey with 100 participants from the ASEAN member states, only 40.2% respondents said that they could trust other countries in Southeast Asia to be good neighbors (Roberts 2012). This trust deficit has hindered the unity of ASEAN and weakened its bargaining power, especially when it has to deal with major countries such as the PRC, the US, and Japan.

Strengthening sociocultural cooperation allows ASEAN member states to familiarize themselves with and get to know more about other countries' culture, norms, and values. It is another way to build trust. Furthermore, a common perception that ASEAN is merely a "talk shop" has spread widely due to its inability to get things done, especially on the noneconomic front.

Fifth, as global demand has weakened recently due to growth slowdown in advanced countries such as the US and the European Union, ASEAN has become more relevant as a source of global growth. Trade has increased significantly among member states and between ASEAN and the Plus 6 countries (Figure 2.1). On the contrary, trade between ASEAN and developed countries has either stagnated or declined. However, as the political relations between advanced countries deteriorate, with major impacts on their trade relations, advanced countries are now seeking stronger trade and financial cooperation with ASEAN. This could be

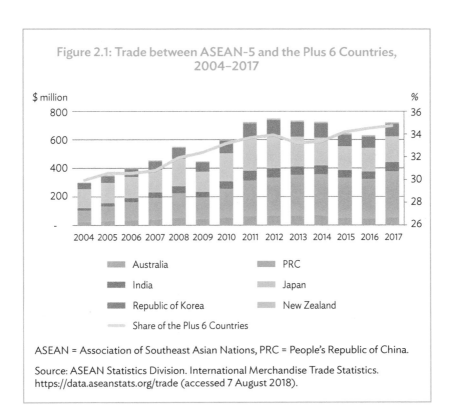

Figure 2.1: Trade between ASEAN-5 and the Plus 6 Countries, 2004–2017

ASEAN = Association of Southeast Asian Nations, PRC = People's Republic of China.

Source: ASEAN Statistics Division. International Merchandise Trade Statistics. https://data.aseanstats.org/trade (accessed 7 August 2018).

beneficial for ASEAN if the member states can manage to put aside their differences and build trust to unite as one voice.

As in the past, in the current context, some ASEAN member states have hinted in closed-door meetings at Indonesia taking leadership. However, on many occasions, this "leadership" has also led to resistance from other group members. As a consequence, this resistance within the organization has held back Indonesia's ideas and proposals—most notably those that are considered to undermine sovereignty and regime security, such as the establishment of a human rights body, a peacekeeping force, a changed decision-making system, and formalized conflict resolution mechanisms (Roberts 2012). Lack of leadership in the current ASEAN structure is clearly a major issue. Indonesia has the potential to lead ASEAN, but should continuously assure other member states that Indonesia speaks and acts for the good of all ASEAN members.

2.3   Indonesia in ASEAN: Future

In 1976, the leaders of the original ASEAN members signed the Treaty of Amity and Cooperation in Southeast Asia, indicating that maintaining peace and strengthening cooperation were the key objectives of ASEAN. Since then, many non-ASEAN countries have signed the treaty. Furthermore, in 1995, the ASEAN Heads of State and Government reaffirmed that "cooperative peace and shared prosperity shall be the fundamental goals of ASEAN." Note that the two key words were peace and prosperity. Maintaining peace within the region over a long period of time is one of ASEAN's major achievements. With this peace dividend, ASEAN member states have enjoyed rapid economic development, which has reduced poverty significantly and increased the standard of living for the people in the region.

The rapid rise of some Asian countries in their military and economic size poses a challenge to Southeast Asian geopolitics and ASEAN's integration. As stated earlier, the 2012 meeting in Cambodia was the first time in its 45-year history that ASEAN could not reach consensus. This underscores deep divisions within ASEAN amid conflicting maritime territorial claims. However, since the PRC, Japan, and the Republic of Korea cannot easily reach consensus, they still need ASEAN. The three countries remain among ASEAN's largest export markets, accounting for nearly a third of ASEAN's total exports as shown in Table 2.3. This indicates the significance of the ASEAN Plus Three trade relationship. Nonetheless, without peace in the region, economic development will stall, and thus prosperity may deteriorate in the future.

Table 2.3: ASEAN's 10 Major Export Markets by Value
and Share of Total, 2017

Partner	2017	
	$ million	Share of Total
ASEAN	585,277	22.9
People's Republic of China	436,833	17.1
European Union	257,389	10.1
United States	233,137	9.1
Japan	217,955	8.5
Republic of Korea	152,538	6.0
Hong Kong, China	106,369	4.2
Taipei,China	105,671	4.1
India	73,490	2.9
Australia	59,049	2.3
WORLD	**2,555,073**	**100.0**

ASEAN = Association of Southeast Asian Nations.

Source: ASEAN Statistics Division. International Merchandise Trade Statistics. https://data.aseanstats.org/trade (accessed 7 August 2018).

ASEAN member states should work harder to build trust for stronger cohesiveness. The common enemy is now the trust issue among the members. They need to work on their differences, particularly on political-security and sociocultural issues. For example, one lingering question often posed is: Is there universal human rights vis-à-vis "Asian values"?

The quality of the current trust building needs to improve. The last decades have shown that with trust as the spirit of cooperation, ASEAN can solve various issues among its member states. In the current changing global architecture of political and economic power, it is of utmost importance that ASEAN regenerate trust and cooperation among its members.

In the future, ASEAN member states will be faced with rising demographic pressures and an increasing probability of being caught in the middle-income trap. To prevent this, it is vital that ASEAN continue to raise the productivity and capacity of its people. This is necessary to climb the development ladder, moving from a subsistence economy to a commercial economy—and then steadily moving out of the middle-income country level of below $15,000 per capita and finally toward a high innovation economy (Figure 2.2).

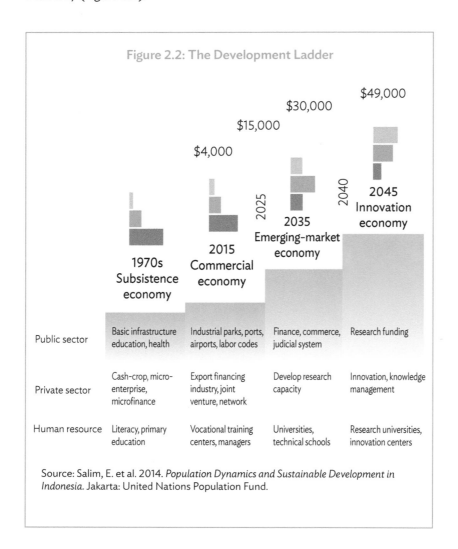

Figure 2.2: The Development Ladder

Source: Salim, E. et al. 2014. *Population Dynamics and Sustainable Development in Indonesia*. Jakarta: United Nations Population Fund.

All this is to be accomplished by keeping each ASEAN member state on the triple track of sustainable development—meeting economic, social, and environmental challenges.

Raising the total factor productivity of each ASEAN member state will require a greater role for science, technology, engineering, and mathematics (Figure 2.3). New technologies and innovative means of development need to take place, changing the customary "resource exploitation path of conventional development" into "resource enrichment value added path of sustainable development."

On this path of productivity-led sustainable development, ASEAN will face new challenges: skills and knowledge gaps. ASEAN needs new economic arrangements that can open ways to strengthen economic cooperation to face those challenges so that no one member state will feel trapped as an object of development of other member states. The road toward social

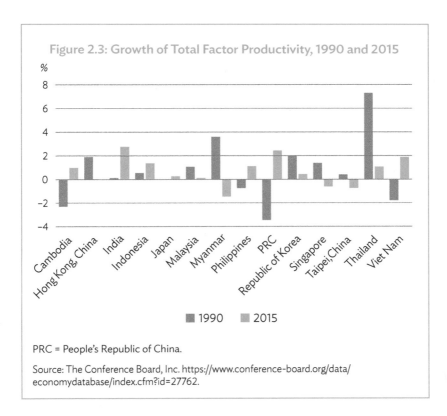

Figure 2.3: Growth of Total Factor Productivity, 1990 and 2015

■ 1990   ■ 2015

PRC = People's Republic of China.

Source: The Conference Board, Inc. https://www.conference-board.org/data/economydatabase/index.cfm?id=27762.

cooperation also needs to be inclusive along the social development path to raise productivity as well as to deal with social inequity and poverty eradication (which emphasizes the need for enhancing productivity-led development).

In the 1960s, ASEAN showed its resilience in weathering the common threat of communism. We shall see again if it is still resilient in facing the current political dynamics in the region. This is because, in the end, each ASEAN member state will realize that amid the current political dynamics in the region, without ASEAN cooperation, this region can easily turn into chaos and instability, as the situations in the Balkans or Middle East have shown.

ASEAN's existence has provided a peace dividend for economic development in the region. Up to now, ASEAN member states have enjoyed growth, security, and prosperity due to the ASEAN arrangement of cooperation and noninterference principles.

Its cooperation needs further enhancement in such a way that the three pillars (economic, political-security, and sociocultural) can raise the capacity of ASEAN as a region to meet the challenges of demographic pressures, the threat of the middle-income trap, and the sustainable growth challenges of the future. This can be achieved through renewed ASEAN cooperation on the path of an all-inclusive productivity-led sustainable growth.

References

Nelson, B. 2013. Can Indonesia Lead ASEAN? *The Diplomat*. 5 December.

Roberts, C.B. 2012. *ASEAN Regionalism: Cooperation, Values and Institutionalisation*. Routledge Security in Asia Pacific Series. Abingdon: Routledge.

Roberts, C.B. and E. Widyaningsih. 2015. Indonesia in ASEAN: Mediation, Leadership and Extra-mural Diplomacy. In C.B. Roberts, A.D. Habir, and L.C. Sebastian, eds. *Indonesia's Ascent. Critical Studies of the Asia Pacific Series*. London: Palgrave Macmillan. pp. 264–286.

Salim, E. et al. 2014. *Population Dynamics and Sustainable Development in Indonesia*. Jakarta: United Nations Population Fund.

Increasing regional cooperation and global integration. The fourth ASEAN Summit was held in Singapore in 1992, during which the ASEAN Free Trade Area agreement was signed (photos from the ASEAN Secretariat Photo Archives).

CHAPTER 3
STAYING THE COURSE: FROM A SOUTHEAST ASIAN COMMUNITY TO AN ASEAN COMMUNITY

Delia Albert

This chapter examines the original motivations for the formation of ASEAN and traces the evolution of discussions on economic cooperation. It highlights in particular the role played by bilateral meetings in building ASEAN's foundation.

Introduction

In 2017, the Association of Southeast Asian Nations (ASEAN) turned 50 years old. For some people, life at 50 is just beginning. For others, life has just reached its peak. For others, still, life at 50 is nearing its twilight years. Certainly, a 50-year-old person has become a lot wiser. But how would a 50-year-old organization look?

This chapter shares the views, observations, and experiences of one who participated in ASEAN's formative years representing a founding member, the Philippines. It traces the motivations and well-measured steps that the Philippines, an archipelago, took to engage with its neighbors and take on responsibilities that would strengthen its sense of security in a region that faced challenges from within and without. It aims to provide context, understanding, and appreciation of the crucial role that leaders of the founding member countries played in transforming the tensions between and among them into relationships built on trust and respect, thus paving the way to a community of dynamic economies.

I was privileged to have started my diplomatic career in 1967 as a Foreign Service Staff Officer and Assistant to the Secretary of Foreign Affairs, Narciso Ramos, a seasoned diplomat with 31 years of experience in public service. He signed the Philippines into ASEAN on 8 August 1967 and laid the foundation for a foreign policy that would have membership in ASEAN at its core. Thereafter, ASEAN became almost a daily experience for me until I retired from diplomatic service in 2010 after serving as the first woman secretary (minister) of Foreign Affairs of the Philippines and in the ASEAN region.

3.1   A Historical Background on the Founding Members of ASEAN

The Philippines, as the first constitutional republic in Asia, declared its independence from Spain on 12 June 1898 and then from the United States on 4 July 1946. Indonesia gained its independence from the Netherlands on 17 August 1945. Malaysia formed its Federated States on 16 September 1963, while Singapore became a state on 9 August 1965. Thailand, which was long ruled by a monarchy, was never conquered by a Western colonial power.

For Southeast Asia, the 1960s were rather troubled years as each of the potential members of ASEAN had some dispute with one or two of its neighbors. Following their newfound independence from colonial rule, there were bilateral territorial disputes between the Philippines and Malaysia over Sabah, between Indonesia and Malaysia over Kalimantan, as well as tension between Singapore and Malaysia after the former's separation from the Federation of Malaya. Insurgencies within the countries were active, some of which continue to challenge authorities to this day. But a common external threat to all at that time was the spread of communism not only coming from the People's Republic of China (PRC) but also from Viet Nam.

A common motivating factor for all the leaders of the founding countries, therefore, was to ensure the security of their individual countries, which could be effectively gained through goodwill and being on friendly terms with its immediate neighbors. For the Philippines, it initially meant engagement with Malaysia.

Determined to patch up differences, the "ASEAN Way" of settling disputes and arriving at consensus, best described as *mushawarah* (consultation) and *mufakat* (consensus), was adopted. This practice or culture has played a major role in keeping the peace and stability in the region and may even serve to explain the "ASEAN phenomenon."

In an effort to address bilateral issues that were unleashed by independence, the Philippines and Malaysia joined by Thailand formed the Association of Southeast Asia (ASA) in 1961. In 1963, Malaysia, the Philippines, and

Indonesia organized Maphilindo. Both organizations were short-lived because of the limited scope of what they sought to achieve.

The following statement of Foreign Secretary Ramos is a clear indication of national policy that the Philippines adopted from the early stages of ASEAN—a statement of support and endorsement of collective efforts to ensure peace, security, and prosperity for the region (Velasco 2008):

> "We believe that ASEAN can provide the key to open the doors of Southeast Asia to the life-giving winds in the 20th century progress. Considering how well and how fast ASA managed to advance in the short period of its existence we can confidently assure ourselves that its child and heir ASEAN, has within it the seed of greatness and the needed potential to meet our highest expectations."

Following the signing of the ASEAN Declaration in Bangkok, Thailand, Secretary Ramos as host of the fourth ASA Conference on 14 August 1967 welcomed his colleagues in Manila as "old friends" where he cited ASA as a regional cooperative organization, which has managed to fill a need of the area. However, at the meeting, he also highlighted the "privilege" to have participated in the founding of a new and enlarged regional organization: ASEAN. He reassured the conferees that ASEAN had been established not to eliminate or destroy ASA, but that ASEAN was committed to continue what ASA had started with wider participation of other countries in the region and a broader mandate.

For Secretary Ramos, ASA, Maphilindo, and ASEAN were milestones in the development of regional cooperation, with ASA as the "pathfinder, the doughty innovator and the inspired pioneer." Interestingly, though he was not an economist, he exhorted members of both group of countries to direct their national energy and potentials toward economic independence through the establishment of a free trade area, the extension of mutual assistance in pursuing agriculture programs, as well as the freer flow of social and cultural contacts among the people of the region.

Furthermore, as a true believer in regional cooperation as a means to achieve peace, security, and the well-being of the country and its people, Secretary Ramos was firm in conveying his conviction that, "ASEAN will survive because it is ours: it belongs to the region."

For him, while ASA had served its purpose "common sense and circumstances demanded readjustments and adaptation to the more stringent demands of the entire Southeast Asian region." For him, the time for an expanded regional organization had come. Ultimately, people and leaders would want to take responsibility for their region's destiny. Meanwhile, their discussions included ways to avoid getting dragged into the competition for influence brought by the big powers who were jockeying for position and influence in Southeast Asia.

To this end, Secretary Ramos conveyed the following message after signing the Bangkok Declaration which reflected both the process and shared vision.

> "The Declaration we have just signed was not easy to come by; it is the result of a long and tedious negotiation which truly taxed the good will, the imagination, the patience and the understanding of the five participating ministers. That the Association of Southeast Asian Nations has become a reality despite all these difficulties only attests to the fact that ASEAN's foundations have been well and solidly laid."

He, along with Presidium Minister for Political Affairs and Minister for Foreign Affairs Adam Malik of Indonesia, Deputy Prime Minister and Minister of Defence and Minister of National Development Tun Abdul Razak of Malaysia, Foreign Minister S. Rajaratnam of Singapore, and Foreign Minister Thanat Khoman of Thailand agreed that it was time for Southeast Asians to build their own community themselves. After consulting and meeting for a year, the ministers formed a bigger group. They designated Secretary Ramos, a known writer, to draft the basic principles on which the new grouping would carry out its mandate. Thailand, which was instrumental in brokering better relations among the neighboring countries, invited the four ministers to Bangkok the following year.

It was people like them, with vision and goodwill, who sat together after a relaxing game of golf in Bangsaen, Thailand, and declared their shared wishes and hopes for the people of the region. Despite the prevailing power play in the region, according to Secretary Ramos, the five men trusted each other. It was this trust that led them to advise their leaders to get to know each other better. This growing trust led to bilateral visits between the leaders. In retrospect, this exchange of visits by leaders enabled them to develop a "comfort zone" on which to build trust.

3.2   Weaving the ASEAN Tapestry

These past 4.5 decades of constant contacts through meetings and more meetings among the leaders and people of ASEAN can be likened to the process of "weaving an ASEAN tapestry." As in a piece of ikat cloth common to Southeast Asian cultures, the more the threads meet and intersect, the denser and stronger the fabric. During this period, ASEAN underwent various phases of transformation from its original design to what it has become today. These phases could be classified under four clusters tagged the four Cs: consultations, commitment, cooperation, and community building.

Consultations

Following the signing of the Bangkok Declaration, there was a period of consultations between and among diplomats and other senior government officials. Because each country had undergone historical experiences under different colonial rulers, which kept them apart for some time, people in Southeast Asia generally knew very little of each other. This was then a period of discovering neighbors as well as themselves as independent, sovereign nations. For diplomats, it was also getting to know their ASEAN counterparts better. Through frequent meetings, representatives from the five countries became more conscious of ASEAN's geography, history, and culture, especially dietary habits, and consequently even acquired a taste for what was formerly perceived as exotic.

However, it took some time to really think and act together as a region. Diplomats still represented individual countries with specific national sovereign interests. Competition for individual bilateral attention rather than group interest was common practice. It was not easy to cross mental national boundaries.

The Philippines as a founding member was a keen organizer and participant in the early days of regional cooperation. Its attempts at organizing groups to address bilateral issues was best described in domestic media as "magnificent improvisation" due to the lack of organized institutional linkages that would provide the much needed public space for consultations and deliberation.

For the Philippines, one of the bilateral issues that hindered accelerated cooperation was the dispute with Malaysia over Sabah. Notwithstanding the tension between the two countries, Secretary Ramos entered into an anti-smuggling agreement in Kuala Lumpur on 1 September 1967 soon after the signing of the Bangkok Declaration. He admitted that there had been difficulties finalizing the agreement and that they had unduly strained the basically amicable relations between the two countries, but he continued to pursue dialogue with Malaysia.

With diplomatic skill and good intentions, he and Mrs. Ramos invited Deputy Prime Minister Tun Abdul Razak and his wife Mme. Toh Puan Rahah to a friendly and relaxing golf weekend in Baguio, Philippines, in December 1967. Senior advisers from both sides were invited also to ensure continuity of consultations. I was privileged to witness the deepening friendship and trust shared by the two ministers on several occasions.

His efforts in strengthening the bonds between leaders in the region was manifested again when he spent some time with Indonesian Foreign Minister Adam Malik to help ease the tension between Indonesia and Malaysia. Somehow, Secretary Ramos felt "at home" with Foreign Minister Malik and came back with anecdotes of close friendship and mutual respect.

This relationship was confirmed recently by Sabam Siagian, an Indonesian journalist who conducted an interview with Adam Malik some time ago. He added that the ministers asked Secretary Ramos to work on the draft declaration to be considered in Bangkok as they held him in high esteem and respected his dedication and desire to engage the Philippines in the region in addition to his writing skills as a former journalist.

All these initiatives and actions have signified the deep interest of the Philippines for a wider and deeper regional cooperation in spite of the existence of challenges to its bilateral relations.

In June 1966, Secretary Ramos actively participated in the Asian and Pacific Council (ASPAC) ministerial meeting in Seoul, Republic of Korea, which was aimed at building a regional community in Asia and the Pacific through cooperation activities in political, economic, social, cultural, technological, and related endeavors.

At this meeting, Secretary Ramos continued to express his conviction that regional cooperation will keep the peace in Asia when he said, "It is for us to decide what the future would be. Either we fortify the fabric of peace in the region through greater cooperative undertakings or suffer the consequences of inaction and indifference in the face of the adverse forces that threaten to engulf us."

Following the founding of ASEAN in Bangkok, the Philippines opened a Consulate in Singapore to prepare for the opening of full diplomatic relations, which were formally established on 16 May 1969 and the Embassy opened in 1971. This rounded up its diplomatic relations with the rest of the five original ASEAN members.

Indeed, Secretary Ramos' efforts in restoring friendly relations between the Philippines and Malaysia is one of the manifestations of his personal desire to draw the Philippines in its search for an Asian identity by forging closer ties with its neighbors. Moreover, the extraordinary efforts of Secretary Ramos to reach out were also necessary to overcome the thorny issue of the Philippines as host to the largest concentration of American military installations in Asia at the time.

Invisible Processes

Notably, many of the written works on ASEAN have remained on the "visible" or the institutions and agreements that seek to explain its dynamics. Having participated in some of the activities during its organizational stages, I have noted some "invisible" or less discernable processes that may have had an impact on the realization of the organization's objectives through informal meetings or consultations, especially in the early stages of ASEAN.

Though unstated in the Bangkok Declaration, the subject of a number of consultations during the ASA meetings was the political and security issues, including rapprochement between the Philippines and Malaysia. This was also included in the talks during the days of Maphilindo, a Philippine initiative to ease the tension between Malaysia and Indonesia.

Some of these "invisibles" were covered in private conversations, which sometimes found their way into the statements of foreign ministers, especially when they suggested that the objectives of peace and security in the region be achieved through intensive cooperation in the economic, social, and cultural fields.

At this early stage, intra-ASEAN economic cooperation could not be fully developed due to the lack or absence of the many preconditions, which at the time were difficult to establish. Each country faced national challenges of getting their economies to move ahead. Industries were at their infant stages and needed the protection from more competitive and more efficient economies. Varying levels of development were also a frequent reason for delayed actions or decisions.

Upon the recommendation of their respective foreign ministers, the leaders of ASEAN began to see the value in direct talks with their counterparts. In a study by Professor Estrella D. Solidum of the University of the Philippines, she reported on 96 bilateral meetings between 1967 and 1981 (Solidum 1982). An avid and keen observer of unfolding events in ASEAN, Solidum was convinced of the important role that leaders played in laying the foundation and in ensuring the future of ASEAN.

She noted that meetings always included general proposals for economic cooperation. These were later passed on to ministers and senior officials. Intra-ASEAN problems that were too sensitive to discuss in formal ASEAN-wide meetings, among them border issues, secessionist problems, and territorial claims on land and water were taken up in these bilateral consultations.

She also reported on the observations made by Japanese researchers on these bilateral meetings, some of which were informal talks undertaken without the trappings of state visits. The visits reveal the intensity and the seriousness of the leaders in building ASEAN while addressing their bilateral issues. She noted them in a monograph entitled "Bilateral Summitry in ASEAN" published by the Department of Foreign Affairs' Foreign Service Institute in 1982 (Table 3.1).

Fresh from the Bangkok Meeting, which appeared to have eased bilateral tensions between their two countries, Malaysian Deputy Prime Minister Tun Abdul Razak visited Secretary Ramos and Philippine President Ferdinand Marcos. At this meeting, the Philippines reiterated its proposal made earlier at ASA to create a "Southeast Asia Council" for regional economic cooperation. The idea of a Southeast Asian University to consist of a consortium of universities with high scholastic standing, including degree accreditation and course equivalent, was also discussed. These discussions may have been the precursors to the ASEAN Economic Community and ASEAN University Network of today.

On economic cooperation, the Philippine economic team proposed institutionalizing complementary programs of industrial development, while expanding marketing opportunities and product standards. The Philippine economy in the 1970s was doing well so that initiatives for intensified economic cooperation were more forthcoming than from the

Table 3.1: Bilateral Visits between ASEAN Leaders

			Number of visits
Malaysia	–	Thailand	19
Singapore	–	Thailand	14
Malaysia	–	Indonesia	13
Singapore	–	Malaysia	12
Indonesia	–	Thailand	9
Indonesia	–	Singapore	9
Philippines	–	Indonesia	7
Philippines	–	Thailand	6
Philippines	–	Singapore	5
Philippines	–	Malaysia	2

Source: Solidum, E. 1982. *Bilateral Summitry in ASEAN*. Manila: Foreign Service Institute.

other member states. In 1971, the Philippines envisioned the establishment of a common market as a goal of economic cooperation in ASEAN. This was followed by the Philippines–Singapore proposal for an ASEAN Free Trade Area (AFTA) in 1975.

To gain support for these proposals, the Philippine President visited President Suharto of Indonesia as the first foreign head to visit since the latter's assumption of office. They focused on strengthening bilateral economic cooperation as well as shared information and views on their bilateral relations with other countries, especially those in the region.

To start with, they agreed to form a bilateral joint commission to upgrade and accelerate the implementation of existing agreements that covered various areas of cooperation. They also expressed their determination to promote the development of ASEAN to enable the organization to fulfill its role in achieving stability and progress of the region.

Likewise, the first visit of Malaysian Prime Minister Tunku Abdul Rahman to Indonesia since the 1966 end of "Konfrontasi" highlighted greater trade cooperation. Soon after Tun Abdul Razak became prime minister of Malaysia in 1970, he too visited Indonesia.

During this time, Tun Razak also visited Singapore's Prime Minister Lee Kuan Yew. He urged Southeast Asia to adopt a joint strategy of its own, referring to collaborative action in addressing problems of the region. The same message was delivered by Thai Prime Minister Kukrit Pramoj in 1972 urging a stronger sense of regionalism.

Meanwhile, the flurry of high-level bilateral visits, which included discussions on economic cooperation, gained international attention so that the United Nations (UN) regional office in Bangkok suggested that a study be conducted on the subject of intra-ASEAN economic cooperation.

The UN study titled "Economic Cooperation among Member Countries of the Association of Southeast Asian Nations" was presented and discussed at length at the meetings of the United Nations Conference on Trade and Development (UNCTAD) in Geneva where the Philippines served as chair of the Group of 77.

The discussions on the report were heightened in light of growing North–South debates in the UN. It was also the time when efforts to establish the New International Economic Order was high on the UN agenda and economic cooperation between developing countries became an important requirement for international development strategy.

The study presented three interrelated policies. First, selected trade liberalization, wherein each country creates a list of items and cuts in tariff in stages while aiming at a free trade area as a long-term goal. This policy recommendation was meant to develop interdependent ASEAN markets through liberalization. A second policy recommendation stipulated that some ASEAN member states jointly allocate and implement several new larger-scale projects. The third policy was the so-called complementary agreements system, in which each country specializes in its existing products.

Meanwhile, the UN report was brought to the attention of ASEAN leaders who saw it as an important reference to address the economic stagnation in the region.

This led to the acceptance of the UN report by the ASEAN ministers in 1974 and later included the report in the agenda of the first summit of ASEAN leaders in Bali. ASEAN agreed to establish large-scale industrial plants, a plan implemented under the ASEAN Industrial Projects (AIP) with financial assistance from Japan. The recommendation to establish preferential trading arrangements was also accepted.

It is noted, however, that the UN report was adopted not only for its content on economic cooperation but also for political reasons. It was agreed that to strengthen ASEAN political cooperation, it was necessary to stabilize their economies through economic growth, which required intraregional economic cooperation. The Declaration of ASEAN Concord (Bali Concord I) reflected this factor when it stated the necessity of economic cooperation for political stability.

Eventually, ASEAN's strategy of economic cooperation as provided for in the Bali Concord I was not exactly what the UN report had suggested. ASEAN respected the concerns, reservations, and objections of some of the leaders to the recommendations contained in the study.

The proposal of the Philippines with support from Singapore for the establishment of AFTA as early as 1975 was watered down to that of a preferential trading agreement. In view of this development, the Philippines proposed an across-the-board tariff reduction of 10%–15%.

Commitment

To continue their quest for peace and stability in the region after signing the Bangkok Declaration, the five foreign ministers met again and signed the 1971 Kuala Lumpur Declaration, which made the region a "Zone of Peace, Freedom and Neutrality" (ZOPFAN). This signified their resolve to keep the region free from external interference. This declaration had a special significance for the Philippines in view of the presence of American bases in the country.

The continued bilateral visits and the subsequent declaration of ZOPFAN provided a form of reassurance that paved the way for leaders to get together for the first time in Bali, Indonesia, where they signed the Declaration of ASEAN Concord or Bali Concord I and the Treaty of Amity and Cooperation in Southeast Asia in 1976. They committed to intensifying cooperation in the areas of economic and social development as well as to assisting each other in the event of natural disasters, in regional development programs, as well as the peaceful settlement of intraregional disputes.

Notably they committed themselves to the development of a recognizable ASEAN identity and the establishment of an ASEAN community—albeit with a small letter "c"—while giving each other time to develop that "sense of community." They also established a secretariat based in Jakarta to handle the growing number of cooperation activities.

It is notable that the early ideas and intentions considered at these bilateral and multilateral meetings have found their way to agreements and institutions which has led to building the ASEAN Community.

The first ASEAN Summit in Bali remains a landmark in ASEAN's evolution as a regional organization. It finally formalized consultations and interactions with a sense of commitment from the ASEAN Leaders. The visual picture of a region moving together as a group was discernible. It also marked the preparedness of officials to harmonize their views and coordinate positions for common actions. The ASEAN Summit signaled a new and more convincing awareness of the importance of concerted actions not only on political matters but more visibly on economic cooperation among themselves both within and outside the region.

After establishing a considerable comfort zone among the leaders, a second summit was held in Kuala Lumpur in 1977 where the leaders focused on intensifying intra-ASEAN cooperation and the formalization of ASEAN's dialogue relations with other countries outside the immediate region. This led to the formation of third-country ASEAN committees in capitals around the world. These third-country committees were especially effective in forging a better understanding of each other's bilateral concerns and strengthened the position of the group vis-à-vis the host country. The third-country committees are especially helpful in capitals where not all of the ASEAN members are physically present, especially in Africa and South America.

Dialogue relations also signified that ASEAN members felt comfortable among themselves and were ready to take on others outside the immediate group.

In the process, a quiet understanding also evolved that the Philippines would take an active role in ASEAN's relations with Latin American countries due to the close cultural ties between the Philippines and former Spanish colonies. In 2004, the Ministerial Meeting of the Forum for East Asia–Latin American Cooperation (FEALAC) was held in the Philippines. This resulted in a better understanding and appreciation for ASEAN in the minds of South American leaders. It also brought two geographically distant groups of nations closer to each other.

Today, ASEAN not only maintains relationships with its dialogue partners but also remains in the "driver's seat" of the ASEAN Regional Forum where political and security issues are discussed. For the Philippines, the ASEAN Regional Forum has been a helpful public space to raise its concerns on the security of the region, especially as it impacts its geographic concerns as an archipelago.

It was not until 1987 or 10 years after the second summit, however, that ASEAN leaders met for their third summit, this time in Manila following the People Power Revolution in the Philippines in 1986. The participation of ASEAN leaders in the Manila Summit demonstrated support for the Philippines following a period of internal political instability. Moreover, it manifested the desire of ASEAN leaders to encourage the new Philippine leadership under President Corazon Aquino.

However, in between summits, the various ASEAN economic and functional committees were constantly meeting, while building friendships and addressing less controversial issues such as those that unite rather than divide the member states.

The five economic committees working on specific issues were as follows: (i) Committee on Trade and Tourism; (ii) Committee on Industry, Minerals and Energy; (iii) Committee on Food, Agriculture and Forestry; (iv) Committee of Finance and Banking; and (v) Committee on Transportation and Communication. These committees became the responsibility of the Senior Economic Officials' Meeting, which was the technical working group of the ASEAN Economic Ministers' Meeting.

The functional committees consisted of the following: (i) Committee on Social Development, (ii) Committee of Communication and Information, and (iii) the Committee on Science and Technology.

Cooperation

The 1992 summit agreement to establish the ASEAN Free Trade Area (AFTA) was a decisive move to intensify intra-ASEAN economic cooperation aimed at integration. Before then, the word "integration" was carefully used in discussions on economic relations as it would imply the loss of sovereign control over the economy of each member state. Moreover, there was always the concern of uneven levels of development where some were in a better position to move faster than others. Certain industries were not too comfortable to give up certain advantages, while some were still being protected either by law or administrative orders.

While the principle of an ASEAN free trade area had taken root among the ASEAN leaders, the decision to sign up was also influenced by external pressures brought about by the challenges of a "Fortress Europe" and a strengthened North American Free Trade Agreement, among others.

The 1992 AFTA scheme agreement, which took effect in 2010, used the established Common Effective Preferential Tariff as a vehicle for a tariff free zone and also removed quantitative restrictions and other nontariff barriers.

Beyond tariffs, ASEAN also entered into relevant agreements to make intra-ASEAN economic cooperation meaningful and effective as it built up to the ASEAN Economic Community (AEC). It included the ASEAN Framework Agreement on Services (AFAS); the ASEAN Investment Area (AIA), which accords unconditional national treatment for ASEAN investors; and the ASEAN Framework Agreement on Mutual Recognition Arrangements. The ASEAN Trade in Goods Agreement has also enhanced cooperation.

The blueprint for the AEC provided for a single market for goods, services, capital, and skilled labor. The ASEAN Single Window was also organized to integrate 10 separate national windows for customs clearance.

In addition to promoting intra-ASEAN cooperation, ASEAN has gone beyond its ASEAN-wide borders and entered into free trade agreements (FTAs). To date, ASEAN members have entered into more than 80 FTAs.

The Philippines has signed an economic partnership agreement with Japan and is undergoing consultations with Pakistan and the United States. Meanwhile, it is part of the ASEAN–PRC FTA, the ASEAN–Japan Comprehensive Economic Partnership Agreement, the ASEAN–Republic of Korea FTA, the ASEAN–India FTA, and the ASEAN–Australia–New Zealand FTA.

In all these moves, ASEAN has been motivated both politically and economically to enter into FTAs to ensure that it is not left out in the global competition for preferential deals and to further progress for the region.

Community Building

It is noteworthy that ASEAN made another landmark decision in Bali, the establishment of the ASEAN Community, this time with a big letter "C." It rests on three pillars: the ASEAN Political-Security Community, which has been an ongoing concern since the first day in 1967 when securing peace and stability was the main agenda; the ASEAN Economic Community, which has been in the making since the AFTA Agreement was adopted in 1992; and the ASEAN Socio-Cultural Community, which includes areas of functional cooperation such as culture, the environment, education, and health.

The ASEAN Charter, which finally gave ASEAN its legal status as an international organization, also defined the ultimate ambition of its founders to be a "Community" as contained in operative paragraph 1, which reads as follows:

> "The charter succinctly declared to promote a people oriented ASEAN in which all sectors of society are encouraged to participate in and benefit from the process of ASEAN integration and Community-building."

Indeed, ASEAN has done very well in ensuring the peace and stability of the region. Certainly the economic dynamism that the region is experiencing today is a peace dividend. In all this, however, ASEAN has to be conscious of its commitment to its people that whatever gains are achieved should reach as great a number of people of the region as possible. It may be too early to give an assessment of the impact of all the initiatives that ASEAN has undertaken in its efforts to integrate its economies and build an ASEAN Community. Only time and an honest assessment can provide the answers.

For this reason, connectivity will play a big role not only in terms of physical connections, by sea or by air, but in the people's mind-set as well. Moreover, ASEAN meetings, of which more than a thousand take place annually, have certainly tightened the ASEAN tapestry.

Taking a long-term perspective, building the ASEAN Community will have to focus on educating not only students but the general public as well to create regional awareness and to ensure the development of that elusive sense of ASEAN identity.

After all, the ASEAN Community is not only about politics, security, and economics. It is also about shared values and all the elements of human security that bind the people of a region. It is about health, education, environment, and a sense that everyone is part of a larger community.

As ASEAN approaches its fifth decade, it is time to take heed of what the visionary founders of ASEAN had in mind, which is to bring the people of the region closer to each other—as symbolized in the ASEAN logo of 10 rice stalks bound together—by shared values of peace in the region and prosperity for its people.

However, it is rather disturbing to note the following result of a survey on the ASEAN Community Building effort:

> "70% of the general public in the capital cities of the ASEAN Member States lacks a better understanding about ASEAN, 81% is familiar with ASEAN by name and 19% has never heard about ASEAN."

Admittedly, ASEAN has largely been a government-led regional organization and may have missed opportunities to communicate and relate with the people of each member state. While officials, especially diplomats, may have been active participants in building consciousness for ASEAN around the world, it is important to widen and deepen the circle of informed people within ASEAN itself.

The lack of awareness especially among both big and small business establishments has led to a degree of reservation and even resistance to the creation of the ASEAN Community, in particular the AEC.

Definitely, the private sector will have to take on a more meaningful and bigger role in building the ASEAN Community. This includes all those in business, which is the engine of growth in ASEAN as in other economies, as well as professionals whose opportunities for jobs have been widened.

In the Philippines, the private sector—among others, business organizations and civil society organizations—played a key role in raising awareness, initiating sessions focusing on the AEC and its impact on the country. As the 2015 deadline approached, the "rush" to learn more about ASEAN became evident. The services of experts to share their knowledge and wisdom with the growing curious and even anxious business community became much sought-after.

Business organizations, such as the prestigious Management Association of the Philippines, organized dialogues and public sessions to acquaint their members and audiences with issues to address in relation to the 2015 ASEAN Community. This included domestic strength, quality infrastructure, revival of manufacturing, good tax structure, productivity, innovation, institutional strengthening, and development of a strong country brand.

In terms of coping with the movement of persons provided for in the AEC, human resources organizations have organized exchanges and dialogues on various professions with other ASEAN member states. This is of particular interest to the Philippines due to the number of available trained professionals ready to take on jobs anywhere.

To address concerns and anxieties of the general public, academic institutions such as the University of the Philippines have been engaged to provide an ASEAN Information Network of the Philippines. The concept is to build a partnership between universities and the private sector to set up a knowledge network to be known as "ASEAN-net."

Another initiative is the formation of an "ASEAN Society," which intends to engage the private business sector, professional groups, and individuals with special experience and interest in ASEAN to share their knowledge and even wisdom in being part of a wider ASEAN Community. The ASEAN Society will also link the public and private sectors and support, among others, the initiatives of the ASEAN Business Advisory Council.

The enthusiasm shown by the general public and the private sector in these undertakings is a positive sign of a growing national commitment to be part of a larger ASEAN Community.

However, some sectors of the business community, notably financial institutions such as banks, are still not convinced of the promise of the AEC. They claim that opening the sector to foreign and/or ASEAN banks will mean bigger challenges for the smaller Philippine banks. The government is allaying their fears. Meanwhile, a recently passed law allows the full entry of foreign banks in the Philippines. This act will prepare the Philippines for the upcoming AEC and ASEAN Financial Integration Framework.

At the highest government level, the Committee for the ASEAN Economic Community was founded in September 2011 to coordinate both the formulation and implementation of the country's policies on trade and other related economic engagements under ASEAN. This is a clear statement of full support for the building of the ASEAN Community.

3.3   Conclusion

The promotion of national interest is one of the basic principles that motivate a leader in pursuing policies that will serve a country and its people. The ASEAN founding leaders were no different. However, they all saw the need and advantage of addressing their bilateral issues to engage with each other to find the peace and stability necessary for the prosperity of the region.

As a founding member of ASEAN, the Philippines has consistently maintained a positive and constructive position in ensuring the success of ASEAN as a regional organization. The Philippines has undertaken initiatives to promote regional cooperation such as forming the Association of Southeast Asia (ASA) and Maphilindo as well as introducing the concept of regional economic cooperation through AFTA following the UN study on intra-ASEAN economic cooperation in the early 1970s.

Motivated further by a desire to keep the peace gained through years of trial, the organization has adopted what has been defined as the "ASEAN Way of addressing challenges—by arriving at decisions through what may appear to be a circuitous way of consensus-building. While this process may have strengthened the core principles of ASEAN of taking into account the concerns of all its members, it is also seen as a barrier to effective integration when members prioritize their own economic and political interests ahead of those of the region.

While geographically located outside of land connections to the rest of the region, the Philippines has consciously undertaken efforts to connect with its neighbors through subregional cooperation such as the East ASEAN Growth Area together with the participation of Brunei Darussalam, Indonesia, and Malaysia.

The next 50 years could build upon what conscientious cooperation has been able to establish: the adoption of the ASEAN Charter, which gave ASEAN a legal personality and the agreement to build an ASEAN Community supported by the three main pillars of the ASEAN Political-Security Community, the ASEAN Economic Community, and the ASEAN Socio-Cultural Community.

Ultimately, it is through this platform that ASEAN cooperation would benefit both the state and the people and build the ASEAN Community.

Building a community means more inclusive engagement of the wider community of stakeholders. While it is true that ASEAN has largely been a state-centric group of nations, recent events have shown the desire and willingness of the wider community to participate in building the ASEAN Community.

This is especially evident in the growing awareness and participation of the private business sector in consideration of the AEC due to the immediate impact of the various agreements on their respective economic activities. For this reason, the pillar of economic integration is seen as driving the process of community-building and integration.

The success of the ASEAN Socio-Cultural Community will largely depend on the active and responsible participation of civil society organizations and their regional networks considering the wide coverage and scope of its blueprint.

Finally, the concept of the ASEAN Political-Security Community provides a comprehensive platform for cooperation among the member states to ensure the security not only of the state but also of the people. It reflects ASEAN's original vision of comprehensive security, which includes broad political, economic, and cultural aspects.

Having achieved a comfortable period of peace, the ASEAN region today is undergoing a remarkable dynamic growth, which is clearly a peace dividend. ASEAN's future is as bright as how and where its leaders will lead it—hopefully in the same manner that the founding leaders set aside bilateral issues and other challenges to its unity, and built the trust and confidence that set the path of ASEAN to reach its present stage. Moreover, if "Community" means an extended period of time without war, then ASEAN has succeeded.

In 2017, the Philippines once again chaired ASEAN as it celebrated its 50th anniversary. I am confident that with all the work that has gone into building the ASEAN Community for the past decades, the people of the region will have become better informed, more knowledgeable, and certainly a lot wiser in building the ASEAN Community.

References

Solidum, E. 1982. Bilateral Summitry in ASEAN. Manila: Foreign Service Institute.

Velasco, M.T. 2008. *"Enduring Legacy" The Life and Times of Ambassador Narciso Rueca Ramos.* Second Edition 2008. Makati City: Ramos Peace and Development Foundation.

Setting the foundation for regional integration. The 9th ASEAN Summit held in Indonesia in 2003 adopted the Bali Concord II, providing the framework for the establishment of the ASEAN Community by 2020 (photo from the ASEAN Secretariat Photo Archives).

CHAPTER 4

THE EVOLUTION OF ASEAN: FROM POLITICAL AND SECURITY CONCERNS TO REGIONAL ECONOMIC INTEGRATION

Rodolfo C. Severino

This chapter provides an insider's view of the evolution of ASEAN cooperation. It examines the process of building the ASEAN Community in a holistic manner, covering all areas of ASEAN cooperation (political-security, economic, and sociocultural).

Introduction

I cannot say that I am one of the "early thinkers" associated with the Association of Southeast Asian Nations, or ASEAN. Indeed, I first came to know something about ASEAN only in 1988 or thereabouts, more than 2 decades after its founding in August 1967. That was when I became, for the first of two times, the ASEAN Senior Officials' Meeting (SOM) leader for the Philippines.

In fact, it was not until I assumed the office of ASEAN Secretary-General at the beginning of 1998 that I could claim to have learned more about ASEAN than what was in the purview and mandate of ASEAN SOM. In practice, what is in that purview and mandate has evolved into things that have to do only with political and security matters or with the sovereignty of member states. In practice, things that pertain to regional economic integration or cooperation have fallen outside that purview and mandate. Also, most of whatever cooperation takes place in the sociocultural area or, in ASEAN parlance, the sociocultural "pillar" is basically the subject of domestic policy and is, strictly speaking, not susceptible to transnational collaboration except in terms of meetings and networking, learning from one another, and cultivating a regional identity that is so essential to fostering regional peace and stability and economic integration.

However, I have done some research, including interviews, on ASEAN's early years for my book, *Southeast Asia in Search of an ASEAN Community*, which I wrote as a member of the faculty of the Asian Institute of Management in the Philippines and then as a visiting fellow at the Institute of Southeast Asian Studies (ISEAS) in Singapore and which ISEAS published in 2006. On this basis, I can say that I know something about ASEAN's early years.

4.1   Two Abiding Aims of ASEAN

ASEAN, from its very beginning, has had two objectives. The first is to prevent the historical disputes among its member states from developing into armed conflict. The other is to keep the major external powers from using the region as an arena for their quarrels. At the beginning, all five founding states were threatened by the rise of communism, then abetted by like-minded external powers. Indeed, the new Government of Indonesia is widely reported to have joined or instigated the massacre of hundreds of thousands of suspected communists. Soon, however, communism ceased to be an armed threat through a combination of changes in the foreign policies of external powers, national initiatives, and regional cooperation, as well as ASEAN members' inclusive response to erstwhile adversaries.

It is remarkable that, among the seven "aims and purposes" that the ASEAN Declaration (the document that for the next 40 years or so was to serve as ASEAN's constitution), only one had anything to do with "regional peace and stability," and that was "through abiding respect for justice and the rule of law in the relationship among countries of the region and adherence to the principles of the United Nations Charter." The rest had to do with accelerating "economic growth, social progress and cultural development in the region ... for a prosperous and peaceful community of South-East Asian Nations" (note the use of the word "community" even in 1967) and with "active collaboration and mutual assistance ... in the economic, social, cultural, technical, scientific and administrative fields." The only thing that the signatories to the ASEAN Declaration had to say about economic cooperation was a determination to undertake more active collaboration in "the greater utilization of their agriculture and industries, the expansion of their trade." They even pledged to "promote South-East Asian studies."[1]

It must be recalled that the formation of ASEAN in 1967 was made possible by the transformation taking place in Indonesia, Southeast Asia's largest country in terms of population, land area, the economy, and activism in international affairs. It would not do for Indonesia simply to join the Association of Southeast Asia (ASA), ASEAN's template-association composed of three future members of ASEAN—Malaysia, the Philippines, and Thailand—and take over most of ASA's practices and structures, at least in the early years. An entirely new association had to be set up not only because of Indonesia's status but also because of its ideological predilections. Thus, Indonesia's highest-ranking point man for ASEAN, then-Presidium Minister for Political Affairs and Minister for Foreign Affairs Adam Malik, invited Myanmar and Cambodia to join the new association.[2] Unfortunately, those two states, like Indonesia staunchly nonaligned, demurred. They were said to be suspecting that ASEAN would be a replacement for the Southeast Asia Treaty Organization, another brainchild of the United States (US) in its web of military alliances. We have to remember that the US was then mired in its Indochina war, although it was showing signs of determination to get out of the Indochina quagmire, and the Cold War generally.

---

[1]   ASEAN's founding document, the ASEAN Declaration of 8 August 1967, reads in part:
       "(T)he aims and purposes of the Association shall be:
       (1)   To accelerate the economic growth, social progress and cultural development in the region through joint endeavours in the spirit of equality and partnership in order to strengthen the foundation for a prosperous and peaceful community of South-East Asian Nations;
       (2)   To promote regional peace and stability through abiding respect for justice and the rule of law in the relationship among countries of the region and adherence to the principles of the United Nations Charter;
       (3)   To promote active collaboration and mutual assistance on matters of common interest in the economic, social, cultural, technical, scientific and administrative fields;
       (4)   To provide assistance to each other in the form of training and research facilities in the educational, professional, technical and administrative spheres;
       (5)   To collaborate more effectively for the greater utilization of their agriculture and industries, the expansion of their trade, including the study of the problems of international commodity trade, the improvement of their transportation and communications facilities and the raising of the living standards of their peoples;
       (6)   To promote South-East Asian studies;
       (7)   To maintain close and beneficial cooperation with existing international and regional organizations with similar aims and purposes, and explore all avenues for even closer cooperation among themselves."
[2]   Adam Malik later became vice-president of Indonesia in 1978.

At the same time, Indonesia was transforming itself from the Sukarno to the Suharto era, from socialism and autarky in economic policy to relative openness to international markets and foreign aid and investments, from the left in foreign policy to a more balanced posture in international affairs.

Malaysia had territorial and other jurisdictional disputes with all of its immediate neighbors. There were occasional tensions between Thailand and Malaysia over several issues, including most prominently some southern areas of Thailand, the people of which spoke Malay and adhered to Islam, rather than Theravada Buddhism, the religion of the great majority of Thais. Indonesia was opposed, militarily and otherwise, to the formation of Malaysia as a British-inspired enterprise. The Philippines was hostile to the inclusion of Sabah, to much of which it had a legal claim, in the new Federation of Malaya. Singapore and Malaysia had recently undergone an acrimonious separation as well as having territorial disputes between them.

It was mostly to prevent these disputes and disagreements from erupting into something worse that ASEAN was formed, through dialogue and consultation, as well as golf games, personal friendships, and contacts.

4.2   A World Divided

It must also be recalled that the world when ASEAN was founded was very different from what it is today. ASEAN was founded in 1967, when the world was divided by the Cold War and, in another dimension, by the need to be aligned or nonaligned. Thus, Indonesia and, later, Malaysia, two of ASEAN's founding members, found it necessary to reaffirm their "non-alignment," while Thailand and the Philippines, another two of ASEAN's founding members, were close allies of the US. Later, however, all ASEAN members, including Singapore, the fifth original member, and Brunei Darussalam, which joined ASEAN at the beginning of 1984, were admitted to the Non-Aligned Movement (NAM). Cambodia, Indonesia, and Myanmar (which in 1979 quit NAM shortly after the summit in Cuba) were original members of the nonaligned and leading participants in the landmark 1955 Bandung meeting; the Lao People's Democratic Republic (Lao PDR) joined NAM in 1964 (33 years before becoming an ASEAN member), Malaysia and Singapore (two original ASEAN members), which had separated in 1965 after an uneasy 2-year merger, in 1970, and Brunei Darussalam, the Philippines, and Thailand in 1993 (the year after Indonesia assumed NAM's 3-year chairmanship). Myanmar rejoined NAM in 1992. Viet Nam is recorded as having become a NAM member in 1976, a year after the country's reunification and the end of the Viet Nam War—and 19 years before joining ASEAN.

In 1971, 4 years after ASEAN's establishment, the ASEAN foreign ministers, prodded by Malaysia, found it useful to proclaim Southeast Asia a "Zone of Peace, Freedom and Neutrality" (ZOPFAN); freedom here meaning not fundamental freedoms as understood in the West and in the 1948 Universal Declaration of Human Rights, but freedom from dictation by the major powers, and neutrality not as international law would have it but in the sense of nonalignment between the "two" Cold War blocs of states. In this sense, Malaysia had become more "neutral" after Tun Abdul Razak, the father of Malaysia's 6th Prime Minister Najib, had taken over from Tunku Abdul Rahman, Malaysia's first leader, in the wake of the May 1969 race riots in the country.

Tun Ismail bin Dato Abdul Rahman, Malaysia's then deputy prime minister, explained Malaysia's motivation for proposing ZOPFAN: "It is with Viet Nam in mind together with the withdrawal of the American and British from Southeast Asia that my government is advocating a policy of neutralization for Southeast Asia to be guaranteed by the big powers, viz. the US, the USSR, and the People's Republic of China." He continued, "The policy is meant to be a proclamation that this region of ours is no longer to be regarded as an area to be divided into spheres of influence of the big powers. It may be regarded as a project to end or prevent small countries in this region from being used as pawns in the conflict between the big powers. The policy of neutralization represents a programme to ensure stability and preserve peace in this area so that we may get on with the urgent task of developing our countries and improving the wealth and welfare of our peoples." The deputy prime minister added, "The tragedy of Viet Nam is a telling testimony to the dangers of big power interference, involvement, or intervention in the internal affairs of small countries. The lesson of the Viet Nam War is clear - big powers should leave small countries to themselves, to evolve their own systems of government and to work out their own programmes for progress and prosperity" (Fourth ASEAN Ministerial Meeting, Manila, 12 March 1971; quoted in Abad 2000).

In any case, in the year of ASEAN's founding in 1967, the Cold War was at its height. Part of it was the US venture into Indochina, with the support of some ASEAN member states. It was in this situation that ASEAN as an association sought to position itself in the middle, although some of its individual member states remained part, openly, or covertly of the US web of alliances in East Asia.

The twin objectives of ASEAN—to keep disputes among members from developing into armed conflict and the quarrels of the strong from involving Southeast Asia—have basically remained the same throughout its almost half a century of existence. Even regional economic integration, although it has its own logic, has, especially in the eyes of some, if not all, of ASEAN's external partners, its own strategic purposes. Whether those strategic considerations have fundamentally succeeded, in the views of ASEAN member states and of the major powers, is up to future events and past history to assess and decide.

Nevertheless, especially at the beginning, these objectives have had to be disguised, as ASEAN wanted to continue to be seen only as an association for economic and cultural cooperation, to avoid being mistaken for a military alliance or defense pact.

Singapore's Foreign Minister S. Rajaratnam, wrote in 1972, "My Government believes that ASEAN should remain an organization for economic cooperation. However, ASEAN countries cannot isolate their economic strivings from the political issues of war and peace that big-power politics will introduce and are introducing into the region." Rajaratnam is said to have pointed out that "the meeting in Kuala Lumpur was not an ASEAN meeting but a meeting of ASEAN Foreign Ministers to discuss a specific foreign policy matter." He is reported to have then proposed, "Perhaps, the time has come to regularise these extra-curricular activities" (Fifth ASEAN Ministerial Meeting, Singapore, 13 April 1972, quoted in Abad 2000).

The ASEAN foreign ministers have had "special" or "extra-curricular" meetings on specific politico-security subjects since then. Thus, ASEAN is constantly being called upon to "resolve" disputes even in cases for which it was not set up. It is often urged to take common positions even on issues on which the member states disagree.

For example, Michael Mazza and Gary Schmitt of the American Enterprise Institute, in one of the more astute observations on the subject, stress: "China's influence aside, the internal contradiction that has for so long characterized ASEAN – namely, vastly different political systems – may be finally taking its toll. The organization has been unable to solve some of the most pressing problems amongst its own members, let alone those involving external states." (Mazza and Schmitt 2011).

Referring to the July 2012 failure of the ASEAN Ministerial (foreign ministers') Meeting to issue a Joint Communiqué because of its inability to achieve consensus on maritime territorial claims, Aileen Baviera of the University of the Philippines, in another astute observation, stated, "By breaking with the established practice of issuing a communiqué, ASEAN sends a message that some members do not recognise the ongoing existence of shared strategic interests. Then, it is right to ask, what is the purpose of ASEAN, and what is the purpose of their being an ASEAN?"

She continued: "If ASEAN cannot speak with one voice, it will struggle to remain relevant. The failure in Phnom Penh not only undermines ASEAN's 'centrality'; it calls into question ASEAN's ability to negotiate with other countries as a collective actor" (Baviera 2012).

However, the progression of ASEAN from purely political and security concerns to a group of countries professing to discern some value in regional economic integration and sociocultural and environmental cooperation as mutually reinforcing is plain for all who are well-informed and observant to see.

4.3   A Legitimate ASEAN Endeavor

In fact, it was not until the first ASEAN Summit, in February 1976, that economic cooperation was officially recognized as a legitimate ASEAN endeavor, despite former Thai Foreign Minister Thanat Khoman recalling in 1992 that "international realities forced ASEAN to deviate from its original path" (Khoman 1992). It was not until early in 1975 that Indonesia's Coordinating Minister for Economy, Finance and Industry Widjojo Nitisastro and Minister of Trade Radius Prawiro of Indonesia went to ASEAN capitals to lobby their counterparts to support them in their proposal to hold the first ASEAN meeting devoted openly and exclusively to economic matters. The first ASEAN Summit, on the Indonesian island of Bali in February 1976, not only set the agenda for the first meeting of ASEAN economic ministers, including the ASEAN Industrial Projects, but also decided its place and date, in Kuala Lumpur in March 1976 (ASEAN Joint Communiqué, 1976).

In terms of economic cooperation (this was before "integration" ceased to be a dirty word in ASEAN), the association at first publicly saw its main mission and function as its member states giving one another tariff preferences on trade in goods and reducing nontariff barriers to them.

They did this through the ASEAN Preferential Trading Arrangements, an intra-ASEAN agreement in which each of the then-five ASEAN member states committed themselves to reducing tariffs on their imports from the others. Although ignored by most media commentators, the agreement likewise calls for the removal of quantitative restrictions on such imports and other nontariff barriers to them, also within certain time frames. The tariff-cutting schedule is largely on track, no doubt helped by the ASEAN members' World Trade Organization (WTO) commitments. However, nontariff barriers have become the means of choice demanded by some sectors for government protection against regional competition. ASEAN economies, like economies elsewhere in the world, are thus prevented from becoming truly and comprehensively integrated on a regional basis.

In this same spirit of protectionism, and eschewing the benefits that regional economic integration is supposed to bring to the nation-state, ASEAN saw industrial cooperation as giving each member a regional monopoly on a certain manufactured product or group of products. Thus, after much negotiation and haggling, Indonesia and Malaysia were eventually allowed, under the ASEAN Industrial Projects scheme, to build urea fertilizer plants in Aceh (Indonesia) and Sarawak (Malaysia), with government protection from regional competition.

Similarly, in 1982, the ASEAN Economic Ministers' Meeting approved the Philippine proposal for a copper fabrication plant, with which the Philippines had substituted its original ASEAN Industrial Project proposal of superphosphates after proposing an ammonium sulfate fertilizer and then a pulp and paper plant, depending, presumably, on the lobbying power of the company or sector involved.

Starting with its soda ash project, Thailand had a similar history of changing proposals. Having discovered deposits of natural gas in its national territory, Bangkok in 1983 announced plans to produce urea fertilizer. Indonesia and Malaysia viewed this with misgivings, of course. The ASEAN economic ministers approved in 1990 the potash-mining project that Thailand had proposed in replacement of the original proposal. For this, the ASEAN Potash Mining Public Co. Ltd. was formed. In 2004, the Government of Thailand decided to pull out of the project, claiming that potash mining was for private enterprise to undertake.

Singapore, with its doctrinal and pragmatic devotion to the free market and aversion to "states deciding what industries to put up for a protected and exclusive regional market" (Abad 2000), nevertheless had originally proposed for itself the manufacture of diesel engines. However, neither Indonesia, Malaysia, nor the Philippines was willing to accept engines below 200 horsepower—nor give up its own plan to set up plants for the manufacture of such engines, which made up the bulk of the regional market.

In 2006, I wrote: "Among the approved ASEAN Industrial Projects, only the urea fertilizer plants in Aceh ... and Bintulu ... have survived as such. No ASEAN country was willing to see curbs on its option to put up industries similar to those allocated to another ASEAN country" (Severino 2006: 217).

I hope I will be pardoned if I quote myself again, extensively this time, in describing what in the early years of economic "cooperation" ASEAN trading and industrial arrangements were all about:

> "The PTA agreement would cover 'basic commodities', particularly food and energy, the products of the ASEAN Industrial Projects and ASEAN Industrial Complementation schemes, and lists of goods to be negotiated among the parties. Implementation of the PTA started at the beginning of 1978. It initially covered 71 products after much hard bargaining on the 1,700 items that had been considered. By 1986, the number of items covered had grown to 12,700 and, by 1990, to 15,295. The margin of preference was originally an insignificant 10 per cent, but was increased to 20-25 per cent in 1980. The cut-off import value was raised from the original US$50,000 to US$10 million in 1983 until it was in effect abolished in 1984. On the occasion of the 1987 ASEAN Summit, the economic ministers signed a protocol committing the ASEAN countries to place in the PTA within five years (with Indonesia and the Philippines allowed seven years) at least 90 per cent of items traded among them with at least 50 per cent of the value of intra-ASEAN trade. The margin of preference for the new items was increased to 25 per cent and for those already in the PTA to 50 per cent, something that the economic ministers had already agreed upon four years before. The ASEAN content requirement would be reduced in five years from 50 to 35 per cent (42 per cent in the case of Indonesia), but 'on a case-by-case basis'; after five years, it could be brought back up to 50 per cent.

Still, intra-ASEAN trade did not grow much. Because the coverage of the PTA was negotiated product by product, the tendency of the ASEAN member-countries, true to the protectionist spirit and import-substitution policies of the time, was to include mostly items that were not likely to be traded (among them; words within these parentheses are later additions of mine). The inclusion of snow ploughs and nuclear reactors became the object of derision within knowing circles. The national exclusion lists were long. In any case, even with a margin of preference of 50 per cent, a PTA tariff would remain high if the most favoured nation tariff was set at a lofty level. Tariff rates were not brought down; those ASEAN products that were covered were only given 25- to 50-per cent discounts on high tariffs. At their 1991 meeting, the economic ministers observed that, while intra-ASEAN trade in items covered by the PTA had grown from US$121 million in 1987 to US$578 million in 1989, it accounted for an 'insignificant' proportion of total intra-ASEAN trade" (Severino 2006: 215–216).

To validate my assessment, I then quote from a 1983 study by the United Nations Industrial Development Organization:

"One might think that ASEAN would move more vigorously on the allocation and establishment of large industrial projects and operations. However, even here, the schemes floundered on the shoals of competing national interests. In March 1980, the ASEAN foreign ministers signed the Basic Agreement on ASEAN Industrial Projects formalizing the conditions governing the five projects previously agreed upon by the economic ministers and other projects to be allocated in the future. (In those days, only the foreign ministers signed formal ASEAN agreements.) The host country would invest 60 per cent of the equity; the other four member-countries would take the other 40 per cent in equal shares. The investor would be a 'shareholder entity' that 'enjoys the support and guidance' of its government. The agreement had provisions on taxation, incentives, the repatriation of capital and remittance of profits, the protection of minority shareholders, pricing, and bankruptcy" (Severino 2006: 217).

It is easy enough, with the considerable help of hindsight, to blame the wrong policies or the negotiators—or both—for ASEAN's unsuccess to integrate Southeast Asia's economies enough to present a serious competitive challenge to the People's Republic of China (PRC) and other continent-sized economies in East Asia for direct investments and export markets. However, we have to remember that, in many ways, ASEAN was a pioneering enterprise and, devoid of experience, was, without meaning to, showing the way to other regional associations of states. Moreover, Southeast Asia's economic theorists were still, in the circumstances of ASEAN's early years, under the spell of economists and practitioners like Raúl Prebisch, the first secretary-general of the United Nations Conference on Trade and Development (UNCTAD) and an influential Argentine economist. Most importantly, the political power of lobbies and special interests has been helping to shape state decisions in many ASEAN countries.

The Private Sector

At first, the ASEAN Chambers of Commerce and Industry (ASEAN CCI), or at least those ASEAN business leaders who had the inclination, time, and resources to devote to regional affairs, was given the authority and mandate, for example, to identify products for inclusion in ASEAN Industrial Complementation schemes. As ASEAN gave up in the late 1980s on trying to manage industrialization and moved toward letting firms essentially decide their own responses to the market, the private sector, except for those business leaders who pushed their companies to reshape themselves in anticipation of the heightened competition that regional economic integration was supposed to bring, was reduced to seeking photo opportunities with leaders and ministers, and thus demonstrating their connections with those in power.

Again with some exceptions, the ASEAN private sector was also reduced to begging for consultation on the formulation of policies that affect their interests or to ignoring government policies altogether. Today, ASEAN leaders and ministers all urge ASEAN to "consult the private sector" on any economic moves that it makes. How extensive and effective those consultations have been depends, of course, on the political system of the country concerned. In any case, it seems to me, there is no such thing as a common position of the ASEAN "private sector" in support of regional economic integration; only fragmented positions favorable to and favored by each company or sector.

4.4   The Challenge of the People's Republic of China

As the 1990s approached, the ASEAN economies were confronted with something that was completely new, but could have been foreseen by the wiser and farther-seeing leaders among them (or their advisors). This was the rise of the PRC as a formidable competitor to ASEAN for foreign direct investment (FDI) and export markets. In 1976, the PRC attracted a negligible amount of foreign investments. By 1992, largely because of the Deng Xiaoping reforms of the early 1980s, this figure had soared to about $11 billion (or more than 6.5% of the world's total FDI flows), and by 2002 to more than $52.7 billion or almost 9%). In comparison, FDI flows to ASEAN (and much of this was concentrated in Malaysia, Singapore, and Thailand) had been overtaken by the PRC, as ASEAN recorded an aggregate of less than $11 billion and slightly more than 6.5% of global investments in 1992. Ten years later, ASEAN attracted a mere $17 billion in FDI, a meager 2.7% of the global total, compared to PRC's share of nearly 9%.

Meanwhile, the September 1985 Plaza Accord—and here I quote myself again—"reached at the Plaza Hotel in New York among the finance ministers of Japan, France, West Germany, the United Kingdom and the USA, had resulted in the substantial depreciation of the US dollar against the other leading currencies. The yen's consequent appreciation prompted Japanese companies to relocate from Japan and invest and establish production chains in the ASEAN countries, contributing significantly to those countries' industrialization" (Severino 2011).

At the same time, the South American trade bloc MERCOSUR (Common Market of the South) was being created, with the Treaty of Asunción being signed in March 1991. The European Union was being envisioned, with the Maastricht Treaty concluded in February 1992. The North American Free Trade Agreement (NAFTA) was being negotiated among Canada, Mexico, and the US. Globally, the General Agreement on Tariffs and Trade (GATT) was being converted into the World Trade Organization (WTO), with the Final Act of the Uruguay Round of Multilateral Trade Negotiations signed in December 1991.

These facts and figures alarmed some ASEAN leaders enough to go along with proposals to make of ASEAN an integrated economy, a highly competitive production base linked with and open to the rest of the world. Thus, on the recommendation of the ASEAN Foreign Ministers' Meeting and the ASEAN Economic Ministers' Meeting in 1991, they decided to conclude the ASEAN Free Trade Area (AFTA) Agreement at the Singapore ASEAN Summit of January 1992 (Severino 2006: 222 et seq.).

4.5   The ASEAN Economic Community

Ten years later, with all 10 of ASEAN's current members on board, they decided to call the ASEAN economic integration enterprise the ASEAN Economic Community. I do not know the circumstances or motivations behind this proposal of Singapore's then Prime Minister Goh Chok Tong. I do not know if accounts of the discussions in this forum were kept in the archives of Singapore's Ministry for Foreign Affairs or of the ASEAN Secretariat. So, what follows on the ASEAN Economic Community is pure speculation on my part. (As ASEAN Secretary-General, I was present in the closed-door forum of the ASEAN Summit in 2002 in Phnom Penh, but not in the unofficial leaders-only caucus.)

I can only surmise that the ASEAN leaders agreed to Goh's public proposal to show the world how serious they were about integrating the regional economy, knowing that only a regionally integrated market will attract the investments necessary for the national development of each member, investments that had been lost to the PRC and, to a lesser extent, India. The only way to demonstrate their seriousness was to invoke the spirit of the European Union, or the European Economic Community, as the most economically successful of all regional associations of sovereign states, although wrongly so in many instances. (I have always maintained that ASEAN will never be like the European Union, nor do its leaders aspire that ASEAN should be anywhere like it; the two associations and the two regions are so different, although the comparison is often made on the basis of exaggerated, if not totally wrong, assumptions about either or both of them.)

Moreover, the 1997–1998 financial crisis, which some Western commentators have labeled "Asian" even if its effects rippled as far away from East Asia as Mexico and the Russian Federation, called into question the strength of the ASEAN economies.

The Blueprints

The Blueprints of the ASEAN Political-Security Community and of the ASEAN Socio-Cultural Community are full of words such as promote, encourage, build, develop, increase, intensify, advance, enhance, facilitate, improve, support, and strengthen, indicating that these communities are never-ending works in progress. These may also mean an acknowledgment that much of the work envisioned in the blueprints is to be carried out by national governments and other domestic entities rather than by ASEAN as a group.

On the other hand, the ASEAN Economic Community Blueprint carries with it a "Strategic Schedule" that commits the parties, in four 2-year tranches (2008–2015), to specific collective undertakings, as "priority actions," within certain time frames. Thus, to help measure the prospects of achieving the ASEAN Economic Community in 2015, as committed, the Asian Development Bank passed to the Institute of Southeast Asian Studies in 2011 the request of the ASEAN Secretariat for help in assessing the situation, then 4 years before its scheduled achievement. The Institute of Southeast Asian Studies, in turn, commissioned global experts to help undertake this task from the points of view of nontariff barriers, services, investments, competition policy and intellectual property rights, subregional development, relations with external partners, dispute settlement, and institutions. In addition, a survey was undertaken to ascertain views on these matters from companies and their decision-makers. The view of the experts and business leaders was unanimous. If the commitments in the AEC Blueprint were to be taken at face value, then the conclusion was inevitable: ASEAN was far from being an integrated economy (Das et al. 2013).

However, as I have pointed out and so has ADB's Jayant Menon, there is another way of looking at this matter—that is, to view it as a measure of how far ASEAN has come since its founding in 1967. One may regard it as ASEAN's recognition of the importance of international cooperation, especially in economic and related areas. One may also look at it as the ASEAN leaders reaffirming their aspirations for and their commitment to the export orientation, reliance on market forces, and openness to the international economic community of their countries' economies. Whether or not one agrees with these elements of the ASEAN leaders' economic philosophies, these are their aspirations and commitments (Das et al. 2013).

4.6   Conclusion

From the above, I conclude that ASEAN has always had two basic aims: to prevent the disputes among its members, territorial or otherwise, from developing into armed conflict, and to keep the major external powers from using Southeast Asia as an arena for their quarrels. Economic integration is a tool toward this end. These aims have had to be disguised as economic and/or sociocultural cooperation, which have eventually acquired a life of their own, as ASEAN cooperation gains in effectiveness. ASEAN agreements are neither self-executory nor enforceable; they depend on individual, sovereign nation-states, and thus on the will of decision-makers in those states, for implementation or compliance. In the light of East Asia's economic philosophy, government-directed "economic integration" does not work, in ASEAN or elsewhere; market forces do.

The ASEAN Community, much less the ASEAN Economic Community 2015, will not bring about drastic, overnight changes in ASEAN's character or ways of doing things. Rather, it should be looked at as a measure of ASEAN's progress from 1967 and a reaffirmation of its commitments to economic openness and to its linkages with the international economic community. ASEAN's external partners in its free trade agreement may have different strategic views and purposes in pursuing and concluding them than those of the 10 ASEAN members.

References

Abad, M.C., Jr. 2000. The Role of ASEAN in Security Multilateralism: ZOPFAN, TAC and SEANWFZ. Paper presented at the ASEAN Regional Forum Professional Development Programme for Foreign Affairs and Defence Officials. Bandar Seri Begawan. 23–28 April. http://www.asean.org/uploads/archive/arf/7ARF/Prof-Dment-Programme/Doc-10.pdf.

Association of Southeast Asian Nations (ASEAN). 1976. Joint Communique. The First ASEAN Heads of Government Meeting, Bali. 23–24 February. http://www.asean.org/news/item/joint-communique-the-first-asean-heads-of-government-meeting-bali-23-24-february-1976.

Baviera, A. 2012. *East Asia Forum.* 26 July.

Das, B. et al.," eds. 2013. *The ASEAN Economic Community: A Work in Progress.* Singapore: Institute of Southeast Asian Studies/Asian Development Bank.

Khoman, T. 1992. ASEAN: Conception and Evolution. *The ASEAN Reader.* Singapore: Institute of Southeast Asian Studies.

Mazza, M. and G. Schmitt. 2011. Weakness of the ASEAN Way. *The Diplomat.* 21 June 2011. http://thediplomat.com/2011/06/weakness-of-the-asean-way/.

Severino, R. 2011. Politics of Association of Southeast Asian Nations Economic Cooperation. *Asian Economic Policy Review.* Tokyo: Japan Center for Economic Research.

Severino, R. 2006. *Southeast Asia in Search of an ASEAN Community: Insights from the Former ASEAN Secretary-General.* Singapore: Institute of Southeast Asian Studies/Asian Development Bank.

Strengthening ASEAN's legal status. The 11th ASEAN Summit held in Malaysia in October 2005 adopted the Kuala Lumpur Declaration on the Establishment of the ASEAN Charter (photo from ASEAN Secretariat Photo Archives).

CHAPTER 5

THE DEVELOPMENT OF ASEAN ECONOMIC COOPERATION AND GOVERNING INSTITUTIONS

Suthad Setboonsarng and Chayut Setboonsarng

This chapter explores how ASEAN economic cooperation has shaped external developments, discusses mechanisms that have enabled cooperation, and identifies challenges and priorities moving forward.

Introduction: Partnership in Dynamic Development

The Association of Southeast Asian Nations (ASEAN) was created during a period of massive change in the international system, when decolonization during the Cold War created tensions in Southeast Asia. Mutual mistrust between the newly independent states was prevalent in the region, which gave cause for concern. There was a risk that miscalculations and conflict would destabilize the region before nation building or economic development could take hold. To avoid this risk and prevent an escalation of tensions, five Southeast Asian countries established ASEAN in 1967 and agreed to work together in creating a prosperous and peaceful region. The resulting stability created the conditions for economic growth and development. Eventually, economics and sociocultural issues became areas of cooperation.

Development and stability underpinned ASEAN's objectives. Peace and security took precedence in ASEAN's formative years. As trade and investment in Asia grew, ASEAN became more focused on economic cooperation. By 1992, major initiatives were taken to further economic integration. After 2015, ASEAN became the ASEAN Community, with the ASEAN Economic Community receiving a significant amount of attention. This chapter examines the historic developments of economic cooperation in ASEAN, explore the enabling mechanisms, and make recommendations for the future.

5.1   ASEAN Cooperation and the Global Economy

Economic integration became an important factor in driving cooperation in ASEAN as the global economy evolved. The ASEAN economies responded to market forces and became more closely linked. Initially, this occurred informally, with the pace and direction of integration differing across the region. Cooperation under ASEAN formalized these processes and transactions, which enabled commerce to expand. The major features of ASEAN cooperation can be understood through a review of the external conditions and the development of regional and domestic markets.

The changes in ASEAN's external environment can be divided into five distinct waves: colonization (1870–1945), independence and nation building (1945–1975), the context of the "East Asian Economic Miracle" (1975–1997), post-Cold War globalization (1997–2006), and, finally, post global financial crisis (2007–present).

Wave I

As protectorates from 1870 to 1945, natural resources were extracted from Southeast Asia. Countries and cities with access to waterways were developed into ports, which facilitated commerce between the colonies and the West. Borders were established between the colonies and the notion of the nation-state began materialize in Southeast Asia.

Wave II

Between 1945 and 1975, colonial powers withdrew from the region following the Second World War, and newly independent countries began the process of nation building and development. There was friction in the region and racial tension at the national level. Various measures and campaigns were undertaken to address these issues, one of which was the establishment of ASEAN through the Bangkok Declaration in 1967. ASEAN successfully abated conflicts and de-escalated hostilities in the region. This paved the way for development, trade, and economic growth. This context of peace and stability allowed the ASEAN member states to participate and contribute to Asia's economic boom in the subsequent years.

Wave III

The period of growth from 1975 to 1992 is commonly referred to as the "East Asian Economic Miracle." The economies of Hong Kong, China; the Republic of Korea; Singapore; and Taipei,China experienced rapid growth and industrialization. The policy mix of open markets, low taxes, and state intervention led to rapid industrialization and the establishment of manufacturing and financial centers in Asia. On a larger scale, this can be understood as partly a consequence of the international division of labor. In a term that visually reflects different levels of industrialization in Asia, the flying geese paradigm of dynamic comparative advantage depicts the catching-up process in East Asia through a regional hierarchy consisting of Japan, the first-tier newly industrialized economies (NIEs) (Hong Kong, China; the Republic of Korea; Singapore; and Taipei,China), the second-tier NIEs (Indonesia, Malaysia, and Thailand), the People's Republic of China (PRC), and other countries in the region (Kasahara 2004).

During this period, Japan led the region as a manufacturing and financial center. As Japan moved up the value chain, it exported these capabilities to Hong Kong, China; the Republic of Korea; Singapore; and Taipei,China. In the electronics, textiles, and automotive industries, technical knowledge and technology were transferred from Japan to subsequent economies, which adopted the industries. This trend continued when Indonesia, Malaysia, and Thailand became a part of the supply chain. As this occurred, investors and expanding multinational companies began to see ASEAN as a single destination. The ASEAN governments responded with accommodative regulatory frameworks and institutions such as the ASEAN Industrial Projects, the ASEAN Preferential Trading Arrangements (APTA), and Brand-to-Brand Complementation on the Automotive Industry. This period also coincided with economic reform in the PRC under Deng Xiaoping, which set the stage for more economic activity in Asia.

Wave IV

From 1992 to 2006, after an interim period of financial crisis in 1997, the ASEAN economies rebounded and adapted to the post-Cold War global economy. The 1997 crisis intensified financial cooperation in ASEAN. Upon recovery, ASEAN member states embraced the onset of the dot-com boom, which heightened demand for electronic and telecommunication products and services. This sustained the flying geese paradigm, as low-cost manufacturing moved to Cambodia, Myanmar, and Viet Nam. Regional cooperation deepened as the ASEAN leaders agreed to further integrate, and new mechanisms were introduced to bring the economies closer together. Some notable agreements include the ASEAN Free Trade Area, ASEAN Comprehensive Investment Agreement, ASEAN Framework Agreement on Services, and ASEAN Economic Community.

Wave V

ASEAN member states were left relatively unscathed after the 2008 global financial crisis. It was a pivotal event and demonstrated that the global economy was going through another rebalancing, with the center and future of growth moving toward Asia. In the current iteration, ASEAN economic cooperation has advanced to a stage where it is increasing engagement with external partners. This can be found in new institutional mechanisms such as the East Asia Summit and Regional Comprehensive Economic Partnership.

Domestic and Regional Market

During the early stages of industrialization, multinational companies formulated regional strategies when investing in ASEAN. Foreign investors saw the potential of a single market and supply chain. Despite cooperation at the regional level, similarities in resource endowments and the generally low cost of labor forced each country to compete for foreign investment.

Workers moved away from the agriculture sector to find employment and opportunities in commercial and industrial areas. The price of food was kept low, while the price of nonagricultural products and services rose through industrial production policies (Setboonsarng 1983). As wealth accumulated in the non-agriculture sectors, a large consumer base for manufactured products in the urban area was created. Governments also invested in infrastructure to support industrialization; this increased the efficiency of trade, lowered costs, and provided the space for automobile demand. A larger and more tangible middle class of consumers increasingly became part of the ASEAN story.

5.2   Evolution of Governing Bodies

The global economy and the strategy of foreign investors informed the ASEAN cooperation process. Regional agreements and mechanisms allowed investors to deploy capital. As the nature of foreign investment changed, so did the depth and direction of cooperation and the governing institutions.

ASEAN began at the initiative of the foreign ministers and reached the leaders' level at the first ASEAN Summit in 1976, where they signed the Treaty of Amity and Cooperation signifying the growing importance of ASEAN. In the early stages of ASEAN cooperation, regional efforts covered agriculture, industry, joint investment, and trade (1970 to 1980s). Decision-makers were committees of senior officers. During the Uruguay Round of international trade negotiations in 1986, ASEAN members found the need for closer collaboration in the international arena. This required a broader political mandate, and thus collaboration rose to the ministerial level. In 1986, the ASEAN economic ministers met for the first time and many initiatives were put forth, notably the APTA. This was subsequently developed and become the ASEAN Free Trade Area (AFTA) in 1992.

As matters of financial shocks and stability grew in importance,[1] the ASEAN Finance Ministers' Meeting became institutionalized in 1996.[2] Nevertheless, financial crisis erupted in 1997. It became clear that even as a group, ASEAN had little leverage over large international funds consortiums. The ASEAN Finance Ministers' Meeting was expanded to include the Plus Three countries (the PRC, Japan, and the Republic of Korea) in 1997. Many initiatives were implemented to strengthen financial cooperation and improve financial security under the ASEAN Plus Three Framework. These included the Chiang Mai Initiative Multilateralization, a $240 billion currency swap arrangement; the ASEAN Bond Market Initiative; and the ASEAN+3 Macroeconomic Research Office. By 2013, the central bank governors were fully integrated into the ASEAN Finance Ministers' and Central Bank Governors' Meeting.

After 2007, focus was placed on the integration of regional markets. The ASEAN economic ministers and the ASEAN Summit increased the

---

[1]   Prior to the attack on the Thai baht in 1996, there was an attack on the Malaysian ringgit in 1995.

[2]   It should be noted that the ASEAN Finance Ministers' Meeting reports to the Summit through the ASEAN Secretariat.

frequency of their meetings, as did senior officers and those at the working level, with an objective of accelerating collective efforts to achieve the goals of the ASEAN Community Blueprint, especially the AEC Blueprint.

Authority and Level of Representation

The increase in the number of ASEAN meetings evinces the growing areas of cooperation. However, resources in terms of human and financial capital—from organizing, preparing, traveling, and hosting hundreds of meetings each year—have made ASEAN more process-driven. Senior officials in each policy area also do not receive equal representation, which hinders decision-making capacity. For example, the Senior Economic Officials' Meeting, which would discuss the ASEAN Economic Community and economic initiatives, convenes at the Director-General level. Meanwhile, the Senior Officials' Meeting, which is responsible for the advancement of the ASEAN Political-Security Community, operates at the permanent secretary level.

Flexibility in the Implementation of Economic Commitments

As the governing bodies and areas of cooperation continued to change, new decision rules and methods of implementation were utilized. The consensus-based system is suitable for making political decisions, such as the addition of new members. However, given the disparity in levels of economic development among the member states, consensus is not the most effective method of advancing ties. Thus, the "ASEAN Minus X" model was adopted for the implementation of economic decisions.

In the negotiations concerning the agriculture sector, countries agreed to have additional flexibility for sensitive products. Member states could list certain goods in a "Sensitive List" for temporary exclusion until they were ready for further liberalization, and a "Highly Sensitive List" where the ending rate is not 0%.

In certain areas where newer members are not prepared to accept dates of implementation, they could opt to be excluded from specific deadlines. For example, measures in the AEC Blueprint will not apply to Cambodia, the Lao People's Democratic Republic, Myanmar, and Viet Nam until 2018.

As issues become more complicated and policy areas expand, it will be imperative for the member states to give serious consideration to new decision rules such as majority and supermajority to allow bolder policy initiatives to move forward.

5.3   ASEAN Secretariat

The Agreement on the Establishment of the ASEAN Secretariat (1976) was an important achievement for ASEAN. From its establishment up until 1992, the ASEAN Secretariat was responsible for providing secretarial support for ASEAN meetings, organizing logistics, and keeping minutes. As cooperation intensified after 1992, it was charged with conducting research and giving recommendations.

The level of professionalism increased to match its needs. Before 1992, the ASEAN Secretariat staff was wholly seconded from member states. After 1992, when it was given a slightly larger mandate, the staff was professionalized and openly recruited; only the secretary-general would be appointed on a rotational basis. In 1996, there were two deputy secretaries-general, of whom one was appointed; in 2002, this number increased to four, of whom two were appointed. In 2005, the staff of the ASEAN Secretariat were given diplomatic status from the host country. The ASEAN Charter (2008) gave the secretary-general ministerial status and the deputy secretaries-general deputy ministerial rank and status.

Although the mandate of the ASEAN Secretariat has increased due to the amount of meetings and areas of cooperation, they are hindered by the lack of diplomatic protocol. This is further affected by a salary scale that has been fixed since 1993. Partially due to Article 30(2) of the ASEAN Charter's principle of equal contribution, the resources available to the ASEAN Secretariat's annual operating budget remain roughly at $16 million.

To further show changes in how ASEAN functioned over time, in 1993 the ASEAN Secretariat had a total of 150 staffers, of which 55 were professionals from the open recruitment system. Staff doubled to 300 in 2015, but only 65 were professionally recruited—up by 18%.

5.4   Performance Assessment

In the last 2 decades, ASEAN's economic growth has been impressive, averaging about 9% annually. This is easily attributed to the peace and stability that was created through years of trust-building.

Single Market

The notion of a single production base as envisioned in the AEC Blueprint has already been realized in certain industries such as consumer electronics, electrical appliances, automotive, and textile and garments. In some cases, manufacturers use ASEAN as a hub to access 20 markets across Asia. Manufacturers also base their regional operating headquarters in ASEAN to support their business operations in Asia and the Pacific. This is further enhanced by ASEAN measures in trade facilitation, such as the ASEAN Single Window and Mutual Recognition Standards. Related initiatives are ongoing as regulatory and industry standards are gradually being harmonized. Trade and investment barriers remain in certain sensitive sectors at varying levels for each member state. For example, agriculture, aviation, and financial services continue to receive some level of protection. However, innovative business strategies and models have overcome these barriers and have created ASEAN companies.

Competitiveness

ASEAN competitiveness has improved, albeit a small degree; its aggregate ranking in the Global Competitiveness Index rose from 55 in 2007–2008 to 50 in 2017–2018, as shown in Table 5.1.

Dispute Settlement

One issue that bears highlighting is the non-use of the ASEAN Dispute Settlement Mechanism. Although this mechanism has been a functional for 18 years, it has not been invoked by member states. Disputes are typically settled through negotiations. This practice does not improve the track record of the ASEAN Dispute Settlement Mechanism, nor does it encourage its use. As ASEAN tries to become a rule-based organization, closed-door negotiations and back channels do not generate confidence in

Table 5.1: Ranking of ASEAN Competitiveness

	2007–2008	2008–2009	2009–2010	2010–2011	2011–2012	2012–2013	2013–2014	2014–2015	2015–2016	2016–2017
Brunei Darussalam	39	39	32	28	28	28	26	-	-	58
Cambodia	110	109	110	109	97	85	88	95	90	89
Indonesia	54	55	54	44	46	40	38	34	37	41
Lao PDR	-	-	-	-	-	-	81	93	83	93
Malaysia	21	21	24	26	21	25	24	20	18	25
Philippines	71	71	87	85	75	65	59	52	47	57
Singapore	7	5	3	3	2	2	2	2	2	2
Thailand	28	34	36	38	39	38	37	31	32	34
Viet Nam	68	70	75	59	65	75	70	68	56	60

- = not available, ASEAN = Association of Southeast Asian Nations, Lao PDR = Lao People's Democratic Republic.

Source: World Economic Forum. Global Competitiveness Index (various issues).

the region's rule of law. However, it should be pointed out that at least one investor-state dispute was settled under an ASEAN arbitration tribunal under the ASEAN Comprehensive Investment Agreement.

Is Prosperity Shared Fairly?

Despite the growth that member states have experienced throughout the existence of ASEAN, one question that should be examined closely is how benefits are divided between ASEAN and its external partners. An indicator of this is the level of intra- and extra-ASEAN trade. Only 25% of total ASEAN trade is intraregional, while the remaining 75% is with its partners. While it can be argued that this is due to similarities in the resource mix of the member states, differences in the level of economic development should encourage labor- and capital-rich countries to trade. Theoretically, if benefits are fixed in proportion to trade, this would indicate that 75% of benefits accrue to ASEAN's partners. ASEAN must attempt to respond to this disparity if the grouping is to be a people-centered organization.

One often cited example is the value chain of the Apple iPhone. Studies have traced how benefits are allocated across the value chain. Figure 5.1 shows that Apple receives roughly 55% of the retail value of its product. The PRC receives a mere $6.64 or about 1% of the total value of the product.

Another major disparity is the level of income between member states. A forecast from the International Monetary Fund's Regional Economic Outlook for the Asia Pacific shows that there is a large and growing disparity in incomes between member states (IMF 2018). By 2020, this will worsen. One of the AEC's objectives is inclusive growth and the reduction of income disparity. This pillar will not be achieved; instead, existing disparities will worsen as more wealth will be systematically concentrated in richer member states.

This is one of the most important challenges that ASEAN faces. There is currently no mechanism that seeks to sufficiently address this issue.

In summary, while the four pillars of the AEC will have different degrees of success, addressing income distribution under pillar 3 should be considered the least successful one.

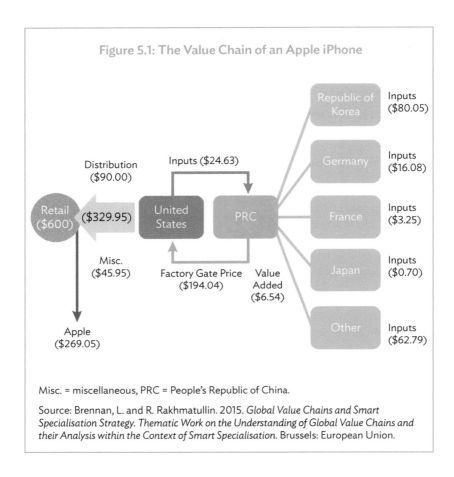

Figure 5.1: The Value Chain of an Apple iPhone

Misc. = miscellaneous, PRC = People's Republic of China.

Source: Brennan, L. and R. Rakhmatullin. 2015. *Global Value Chains and Smart Specialisation Strategy. Thematic Work on the Understanding of Global Value Chains and their Analysis within the Context of Smart Specialisation.* Brussels: European Union.

5.5   Current Practice

ASEAN member states favor a ministerial-led mechanism with the ASEAN economic ministers overseeing much of economic integration. Foreign businesses have consultations with sector ministers; for example, medical and pharmaceutical companies have dialogues with the ASEAN health ministers and make sector requests in this forum. This mechanism has been successful for foreign companies, and so ASEAN companies should become more active in the process.

The ministerial mechanism that consults with the private sector on minor issues may not be an efficient use of the meetings' time and can burden ministerial meetings with regulatory issues. This task could be delegated to the ASEAN Secretariat, which then reports issues to ministers. The recommendation to empower the ASEAN Secretariat is not novel. However, the circumstances under which they were first proposed have changed, increasing the urgency of policy action.

Allocating the appropriate resources to the ASEAN Secretariat and building stronger institutions are critical, at a time when ASEAN rests in the center of Asia's growth story and has more opportunity to make meaningful and lasting contributions to regional affairs. Commitment and dedication to regional cooperation will yield domestic returns as the member states gain more prominence in the world.

5.6   Going Forward

In the next 10 years, there are five parameters that ASEAN should take into consideration, not as challenges to respond to, but as opportunities to position the region for future generations.

By 2020, Asia will be the largest regional economy in the world. As part of Asia, ASEAN has to define its strategic position clearly to work hand in hand with regional partners, taking into consideration the following megatrends:

(i) Trade between Northeast Asia and the rest of Asia is expanding rapidly, and ASEAN will be the junction of this trade.

(ii) Asia will account for 50% of global population growth. To feed, shelter, educate, and care for this population can pose either threats or opportunities for ASEAN.

(iii) Over 60% of the global middle class will be in Asia.

(iv) More global businesses will migrate to Asia, as the economic recovery in the developed countries remains underwhelming in the next few years.

(v) Cross-border business models are changing to take advantage of liberal investment regimes. For example, businesses are quickly embracing new communication technology to support market expansion to include rural populations.

(vi) As a consequence, ASEAN should have a clear position for the region 10 years from now, bearing in mind that working closer together is the only way.

A more people-centered target should be set to address income distribution issues. With strategic and policy foresight, new instruments and mechanism can be implemented to obtain these goals. For example, ASEAN should aim to have the poorest 10% of the population attain an average income of $30,000 per family by 2020. Other goals should include:

- prioritizing financial inclusion and literacy to promote moderate spending, wise investments, and entrepreneurship that would induce change from the bottom up;
- adjusting ASEAN institutions to enable freer movement of capital and people across the border; and
- increasing the involvement of large-scale private businesses. Through cooperation and guidance, a cross-border program could be implemented to encourage joint investments for small and medium-sized enterprises or micro-venture capital. The private sector should embrace this income target, not the government.

On institutions, the ASEAN Secretariat should play a more active role in coordinating the implementation of work plans to achieve this income target. This will need to be accompanied by decision-making rules that are flexible for economic matters, especially those that concern income distribution.

5.7   Conclusion

Economic cooperation in ASEAN has evolved over the years. Changes in the nature and level of cooperation were largely driven by the external economic environment. Investors quickly identified the advantages of a labor- and resource-abundant ASEAN. Member states adapted policies to channel foreign direct investment into the region. An element of competition was persistent, as member states competed for foreign capital. As globalization advanced to a stage where industries demanded efficient supply chains, the investment strategy shifted to utilizing ASEAN as a production base. ASEAN responded to market forces and recalibrated the region's regulatory environment to facilitate the establishment and operation of distribution and supply chains.

ASEAN's decision rules and mechanisms evolved alongside these changes. There was notable commitment from the member states in this regard, as decision rules were amended. This is further illustrated by an expansion in the responsibilities and professionalism of the ASEAN Secretariat, which was necessitated by the deepened areas of cooperation.

As ASEAN enters a new normal in the global economy, there has been a marked increase in ASEAN's engagement with external partners and cooperation in new policy areas. This, however, has not been accompanied by necessary institutional mechanisms that would allow meaningful deliverables from the member states.

ASEAN must give due attention to reforming its institutions and governing bodies. The levels of representation at senior-level meetings should undergo thorough reassessment and examination. Recommendations to increase resources and authority of the ASEAN Secretariat should be quickly implemented.

As history has shown, continuous adaptation and reform have greatly benefited ASEAN. In its current state, where ASEAN has grown in its own capacity, the future trajectory of regional cooperation should include a strategic element that can strengthen resilience, increase competitiveness, and ensure that the people of ASEAN are the primary beneficiary of the region's integration efforts.

References

Brennan, L., and R. Rakhmatullin. 2015. *Global Value Chains and Smart Specialisation Strategy. Thematic Work on the Understanding of Global Value Chains and their Analysis within the Context of Smart Specialisation.* Brussels: European Union.

International Monetary Fund. 2018. *Regional Economic Outlook 2018: Asia Pacific Good Times, Uncertain Times: A Time to Prepare.* Washington, DC: IMF.

Kasahara, S. 2004. The Flying Geese Paradigm: A Critical Study of its Application to East Asian Regional Development. *UNCTAD Discussion Paper* No. 169. April 2004. Geneva: UNCTAD.

Setboonsarng, S. 1983. Pricing Agricultural Commodities Under Policy Constraints with Reference to Thailand. PhD dissertation, University of Hawaii.

World Economic Forum. Global Competitiveness Index (various issues).

Advancing the ASEAN Economic Community. At the 13th ASEAN Summit in Singapore in 2007, ASEAN Leaders endorsed the ASEAN Economic Community Blueprint, setting the goals for regional economic integration (photos from the ASEAN Secretariat Photo Archives).

CHAPTER 6

SINGAPORE'S PARTICIPATION IN EVOLVING ASEAN ECONOMIC COOPERATION AND INTEGRATION

Chia Siow Yue

This chapter explores Singapore's experience and role in ASEAN cooperation. It also touches on broader trade issues, including the effectiveness of ASEAN's free trade agreements, and options for deepening economic integration.

Introduction

The ASEAN Economic Community was officially realized as of December 2015. Hence, it is fitting to be retrospective and assess how far economic cooperation and integration in the Association of Southeast Asian Nations (ASEAN) have come since the founding of ASEAN in 1967 and the first attempts at economic cooperation in 1977. Critics look at the glass as half empty while ASEAN advocates look at the glass as half full.

Critics point to the AEC's unfulfilled promise of a single market and production base, a competitive economic region, equitable economic development, and integration into the global economy. The AEC Scorecard highlighted the areas where the AEC Blueprint has yet to be fully implemented. Advocates argue that ASEAN economic cooperation and integration have come a long way since the 1970s. Economic integration was not on the minds of ASEAN's founders, who were preoccupied with attaining peace and security in Southeast Asia so that individual member states could focus their energies on national economic development. Economic integration and free trade agreements (FTAs) were then taboo words in the ASEAN lexicon. Yet, internal dynamics and external developments pressure ASEAN toward economic cooperation and integration. The AEC is an ambitious integration project and while the objectives, actions, and measures were not all to be achieved by the end of 2015, we are moving in the right direction.

6.1   Understanding Singapore's Foreign Policy and Trade Policy since the 1960s

Singapore's Foreign Policy since Political Independence

In the mid-1960s, politically independent Singapore suffered from a severe sense of geopolitical and economic vulnerability attributable to its geographic location between two much larger neighbors, its ethnic diversity with a Chinese majority, and its small size and dearth of natural resources.[1]

Desker and Osman (2006) maintain that the need for survival, the balance of power, and the globalization paradigm remain the three key thrusts of Singapore's foreign policy that have guided the country in its dealings with external actors.

The late S Rajaratnam was tasked with framing independent Singapore's foreign policy. Survival was uppermost:

> "In a nutshell, our problem is how to make sure that a small island with a teeming population and no natural resources to speak of, can maintain, even increase, its living standards and also enjoy peace and security in a region marked by mutual jealousies, internal violence, economic disintegration and great power conflicts....We shall try to do this by establishing friendly relations with all countries, particularly those nearest to us as well as by ensuring that our foreign and our defence policy do not increase tensions and fears among our neighbours" (Desker and Osman 2006: 4–5).

Rajaratnam believed that Singapore needed to move beyond being a regional entrepôt to become a key node in a globalized environment. He articulated in February 1972 his vision of the Singapore Global City:

> "If we view Singapore's future not as a regional city but as a Global City then the smallness of Singapore, the absence of a hinterland, or raw materials and a large domestic market are not fatal or insurmountable handicaps. It would explain why, since independence, we have been successful economically and, consequently, have ensured political and social stability" (Desker and Osman 2006: 6).

---

[1]   This section draws mainly on Desker and Osman (2006).

Rajaratnam also espoused the need to maintain a balance of power in the Southeast Asian region to ensure the independent position of Singapore. Hence Singapore's policy of welcoming various powers, such as the United States to counterbalance the influence of the former Soviet Union. During the Cold War years and the rise of the People's Republic of China (PRC) as a power in Asia and the Pacific (Desker and Osman 2006: 7).

Understanding Singapore's Trade Policy since Independence in 1965

Singapore maintains a trade policy of minimal import and export restrictions and an industrial policy of export-orientation and free foreign direct investment (FDI) inflows. Singapore's trade policy goals are threefold. First, it aims to expand the international economic space for Singapore-based companies. Second, it seeks a predictable and fair trading environment for Singapore-based companies by supporting a rules-based multilateral trading system. Third, it strives to minimize obstacles to the flow of imports by continuously improving Singapore's trade and business environment. Singapore achieves these goals by engaging its trade partners at the multilateral, regional, and bilateral levels, and working domestically to improve the flow of goods, services, and investments into Singapore.

Since independence in August 1965, the Singapore economy has been transformed from a regional entrepôt into an export manufacturing platform and services hub, and further into a knowledge-based economy. The government played a crucial role in guiding Singapore's rapid economic transformation. Policy focus has been on creating an export- and FDI-led economy, with emphasis on investments in physical infrastructure and human capital; maintaining macroeconomics and industrial relations stability; and ensuring a pragmatic, efficient, and honest and meritocratic government.

Singapore has been a free port for most of its modern history. There was a brief period (1960–1965) when import tariffs were introduced during its "Malaysian interlude." With political independence in 9 August 1965, Singapore rapidly reverted to its free trade position. By the mid-1970s, the only remaining import tariffs were on alcohol and tobacco, petroleum products, and motor vehicles, with limited tariff lines maintained to restrict social consumption, support government revenue, and protect the environment as well as for tariff bargaining under the Agreement on ASEAN Preferential Trade Arrangements (APTA). The General Agreement on Tariffs and Trade (GATT) Trade Policy Review of Singapore for 1992 found that some 96% of all merchandise imports were tariff-free. These tariffs, however, were completely abolished in January 1994 as part of Singapore's tariff concessions in the Uruguay Round. Only six tariff lines on alcoholic beverages remain, and these are subject to specific rates. However, these tariffs have been removed for imports from FTA partners. Singapore also has few import restrictions: import bans are imposed on a few products for reasons of national security and public safety, and as commitments under international conventions; import licensing is required for some products for health, safety, and security reasons, with a special import licensing system enforced on rice.

While Singapore practices free trade in goods, it is less open on services. However, unilateral services trade liberalization has accelerated in recent decades, in line with the objective of consolidating and enhancing Singapore's position as a regional services hub. In financial services, the remaining banking restriction is on foreign access to domestic retail banking. In telecommunication services, liberalization began in 2000, in anticipation of the liberalization required under the World Trade Organization (WTO). This has led to a considerable increase in the number of service providers and a sharp drop in telecommunication charges. In health services, Singapore is liberalizing to become a health services hub, with increased recognition of foreign qualifications. In legal services, there has been an opening up of Singapore's domestic legal services regime and increased flexibilities for foreign and local law firms to offer legal services jointly. Education services are also increasingly open to foreign participation.

Singapore is well known for its liberalization of FDI, particularly in manufacturing. FDI in services is rapidly being liberalized. In 1999, a 40% foreign shareholding restriction on local banks and a 70% limit on foreign ownership of the Stock Exchange of Singapore members were removed, while in 2000, all foreign investment restrictions in the telecommunication sector were removed. However, foreign investment limits continue to be maintained in mass media. The high-openness to FDI, particularly multinational corporations (MNCs), contributed to Singapore's economic upgrading and efficiency, but had the negative effect of leaving local enterprises trailing behind, with the former competing for government policy attention and domestic land and human sources.

Singapore's competition regime has been strengthened with the enactment and implementation of the Competition Law, although a number of areas are still exempt from competition rules and state-owned enterprises or government-linked companies dominate many economic sectors. It has also enforced intellectual property rights protection, including on counterfeit goods. Singapore is also a signatory to the WTO Government Procurement Agreement, and government procurement is also included in many of its bilateral FTAs.

Singapore and Bilateral FTAs

In the past 2 decades, Singapore has been highly proactive in seeking bilateral FTAs. Its bilateral FTA strategy initially raised many concerns and criticisms in ASEAN and beyond.[2] Many trade economists are against all regional trading arrangements, be it the North American Free Trade Agreement (NAFTA), ASEAN Free Trade Agreement (AFTA), or bilateral, as these are seen to be discriminatory and resource-distorting, undermine the WTO, and create a messy "spaghetti bowl" of rules of origin (ROOs). However, since Singapore practices free and nondiscriminatory trade in goods (with largely zero most favored nation [MFN] applied tariffs) it has minimal trade-diversion effects. Some ASEAN economists have also expressed opposition to Singapore's bilateral FTAs, arguing that these undermine ASEAN solidarity, provide a backdoor entry to ASEAN markets, and set a bad example by allowing a big power (Japan) to exclude the agriculture sector. The criticism of the backdoor entry to ASEAN markets ignores the reality of the AFTA ROOs. In any case, some of these criticisms have become muted as more ASEAN member states also engage in bilateral FTAs and ASEAN started pursuing ASEAN+1 FTAs.

Bilateral Free Trade Agreement Motivations
FTAs are instruments of Singapore's foreign policy as well as economic policy. They help to consolidate political and economic relations with selected countries.

There are a number of economic motivations for bilateral FTAs. First, the network of FTAs is aimed at opening up markets for Singapore's exports of manufactures and services, as well as reinforcing Singapore as a regional services hub; attracting more FDI into Singapore's manufacturing and services sectors; and ensuring national treatment, preferential treatment, and legal protection for Singapore's investments abroad. Second, Singapore found the pace of trade and investment liberalization and facilitation in the

---

[2]   For more details, see Chia (2011).

WTO, ASEAN, and the Asia-Pacific Economic Cooperation (APEC) forum too slow and negotiations too protracted to address its economic interests. Bilateral FTAs with selected and like-minded countries produce faster and deeper results. Third, to achieve improved and more secure market access, Singapore's exports of manufactures are FDI-linked and FDI-led. FDI is dependent on export market access as Singapore's domestic market is too small. Singapore negotiates for market access in its FTAs not only for Singaporean exporters but also for foreign multinational corporations based in Singapore. Fourth, to develop an integrated manufacturing center in the region, ROOs in Singapore's FTAs are designed to recognize the integrated nature of manufacturing, where production is outsourced to low-cost centers, but initial research and development (R&D) and the final stages of high-end processing are undertaken in Singapore. Fifth, to nurture a knowledge-based economy, intellectual property rights are enhanced through raising Singapore's intellectual property standards and sophistication. Greater cooperation in the area of science and technology would boost R&D in high-value industries. Sixth, liberalization of services sectors both at home and in markets of FTA partners will spur the growth of Singapore as a services hub.

Singapore negotiators are mindful that they have little to offer in terms of market access for goods, as its small domestic market is already 99% open (except for import tariffs and/or excise taxes on alcoholic beverages, tobacco products, motor vehicles, and petroleum products and biodiesel blends). However, Singapore has some bargaining chips. First, although small in geographical and population size, Singapore has the highest per capita gross national product in ASEAN, one of the largest nominal gross national product, and the largest trade volume. Also, it is a major gateway to Southeast Asia, Northeast Asia, and South Asia. It has a pro-business and pro-FDI environment and an efficiently functioning and non-corrupt government and a non-xenophobic cosmopolitan society. English is the common language of government, business, and education. Second, Singapore's services sectors have only been partially liberalized, and offer opportunities for its FTA partners well ahead of its commitments under the General Agreement on Trade in Services (GATS). Singapore is prepared to open up its services to its FTA partners in exchange for market access in goods, for example in its FTA with the US.

Bilateral Free Trade Agreement Features
In negotiating bilateral FTAs, Singapore is committed to the provisions of GATT Article XXIV and GATS V, rather than the "enabling clause" meant for developing countries.

WTO-consistent and WTO-plus: The bilateral FTAs are WTO-consistent in that they cover substantially all trade, liberalize within a 10-year time frame, and do not raise barriers against non-FTA partners, thus conforming to the requirements of GATT Article XXIV and GATS V. They are also WTO-plus as they encompass free trade in goods beyond its bound tariffs in the WTO (while Singapore's MFN bound tariffs are not zero, they are bound at zero in its bilateral FTAs); liberalize services beyond its GATS commitments; liberalize investments beyond the Agreement on Trade-Related Investment Measures; enforce protection of intellectual property beyond the Agreement on Trade-Related Aspects of Intellectual Property Rights; and provide for government procurement beyond the limits under the General Procurement Agreement. Its FTAs also cover the "Singapore issues" which are not on the Doha Agenda, as well as include commitments on labor and environmental standards. Development cooperation is also an integral part of the FTAs, including cooperation in areas such as development of research, education and training, infrastructure, entrepreneurship, and small and medium-sized enterprises (SMEs).

Rules of origin: In some bilateral FTAs, ROOs reflect the realities of global and regional production networks as they incorporate outward processing and an integrated sourcing initiative beyond the conventional substantial transformation criteria.

Diverse geographical scope: FTA partners are not defined by geographical propinquity. It started with ASEAN but has since extended to other regions of the world. With the revolution in transportation and telecommunication, geographical distance is no longer the trade barrier it used to be. Cross-regional motivations include enhancing and/or consolidating political ties, gaining entry into other FTA markets, or securing access to major markets (the US, Western Europe, Japan, the PRC, India).

Complementary and competing: Singapore has been singularly successful in its FTA negotiations, usually reaching successful conclusion in record time because Singapore has few sensitive exclusion lists, and its exports do not threaten the agriculture of its FTA partners. Singapore is not protecting its labor-intensive industries as it promotes continuous industrial upgrading and faces labor shortages. Singapore is also prepared to open its services to external competition. Singapore's FTA partners include the rich industrialized economies of the US, the European Union (EU), and Japan, as well as the developing economies of the PRC, India, and Southeast Asia. Economic complementarity between north–south economies and south–south economies facilitate both inter-industry and intra-industry trade.

Bilateral Free Trade Agreement Benefits

In many countries, including some in ASEAN, a major benefit of participation in an FTA is that it pressures domestic reforms and prevent their reversal (since FTA commitments are binding). In Singapore, economic reforms are unilaterally undertaken and usually in advance of international and regional agreements.

The main FTA beneficiaries are Singapore-based companies (both domestic and foreign), goods exporters, service providers, and investors, all of whom gain from the liberalization of trade in goods and services, investment, and government procurement, and better IP protection. Singapore consumers benefit little from cheaper imports since almost all imports already enter Singapore duty-free. However, trade in services liberalization leads to inflow of foreign service providers, which improves efficiency as well as range and quality of services available to consumers. There are also indirect benefits as trade expands and more FDI flows into Singapore, creating jobs and spin-offs for domestic industries. FTAs also serve as superhighways that connect Singapore to major economies and new markets.

Singapore's network of FTAs is designed to position the country as an integrated manufacturing center, promote R&D, and drive the services hub.

A study by Titus Lee and colleagues (2011) evaluates the impact of FTAs in force at the end of 2008, with the FTA partners accounting for $182 billion or nearly 30% of Singapore's total domestic exports. The study distinguished the export effects of Singapore's bilateral FTAs and plurilateral FTAs. By reducing tariffs, exports originating from Singapore may now be cheaper and thus more competitive relative to the partner country's own products and exports of other countries. Hence, bilateral FTAs are unambiguously expected to increase Singapore's domestic exports. For plurilateral FTAs, the export effects are more ambiguous. When Singapore signs an FTA with two or more countries, it may result in increased trade between its FTA partners, and the FTA would lead to reduced domestic exports from Singapore. This could occur for Singapore in its bilateral FTAs with Japan and the Republic of Korea simultaneously coexisting with the ASEAN–Japan and ASEAN–Republic of Korea FTAs. The study's modeling results confirm that FTAs generally contributed positively to Singapore's domestic exports.

Singapore's Free Trade Agreement Partners
Singapore's network of FTAs now includes 22 bilateral and regional FTAs in force. The EU–Singapore FTA was concluded in December 2012 and has yet to be ratified by the European Parliament.

Table 6.1 shows the list of Singapore's FTA partners while Table 6.2 shows the MFN tariff rates of Singapore's FTA partners.

United States–Singapore Free Trade Agreement
The US–Singapore FTA (USSFTA) is of particular interest to Singapore given the size of the US market and the agreement's scope. The USSFTA is extremely complex and contains several WTO-plus provisions. It has over 1,400 pages (250 pages of text and 1,200 pages of annexes) and 21 chapters and was concluded on 15 January 2003. There are economic and strategic reasons for the USSFTA on both sides. At the time of negotiations, the US was Singapore's major trading partner, investor, and source of technology and management know-how. There were about 1,300 US companies in Singapore, many of them using Singapore as a base to export to the region and beyond as well as back to the US. Singapore also views the US as playing an important strategic role in regional peace and stability.

Tariffs and import restrictions: It is no "giveaway" for Singapore to commit to immediate zero tariffs on all US goods, including alcoholic beverages. However, unlike Singapore's zero MFN applied tariffs in the WTO, these zero tariffs are binding. A crucial objective for Singapore is to gain preferential zero-tariff access into the US market. US tariffs are phased out in stages, with 92% of products enjoying immediate zero tariffs, and the remaining 8% of tariffs phased out over a 10-year period. By sector, major beneficiaries in Singapore are chemicals, petrochemicals, electronics, instrumentation equipment, processed foods, and mineral products. Across sectors, the major beneficiaries are the US multinational corporations in Singapore, as they accounted for over 60% of Singapore's merchandise exports to the US in 2000. A clear Singapore objective is to anchor US multinational corporations in Singapore.

Rules of origin and the Integrated Sourcing Initiative: There are three general origin rules: change in tariff classification, local or regional value content, and process rules. The USSFTA uses a product-specific approach, with each product having a separate and distinct ROO. The most commonly used is the product transformation at the six-digit level. Manufacturing in Singapore makes heavy use of outward processing. For example, parts and components are shipped from Singapore to another country for

Table 6.1: Singapore's Free Trade Agreement Partners

REGIONAL	Entry into force	BILATERAL	Entry into force
1 ASEAN Free Trade Area (AFTA)	1993	1 New Zealand–Singapore Comprehensive Economic Partnership (NZSCEP)	2001
ASEAN Framework Agreement on Services (AFAS)	1995		
ASEAN Investment Area (AIA)	1998		
2 ASEAN–China Free Trade Area (ACFTA)	2005–2009	2 Japan–Singapore Economic Partnership Agreement (JSEPA)	2002
3 ASEAN–Korea Free Trade Area (AKFTA)	2007–2009	3 Singapore–Australia Free Trade Agreement (SAFTA)	2003
4 ASEAN–Japan Comprehensive Economic Partnership Agreement (AJCEPA)	2009	4 US–Singapore Free Trade Agreement (USSFTA)	2004
5 ASEAN–Australia–New Zealand Free Trade Area (AANZFTA)	2010	5 India–Singapore Comprehensive Economic Cooperation Agreement (CECA)	2005
6 ASEAN–India Free Trade Area (AIFTA)	2009–2014	6 Singapore–Jordan Free Trade Agreement (SJFTA)	2005
7 ASEAN–Hong Kong, China FTA (AHKFTA)	signed 2017	7 Korea–Singapore Free Trade Agreement (KSFTA)	2006
8 EFTA–Singapore Free Trade Agreement (ESFTA)	2003	8 Panama–Singapore Free Trade Agreement (PSFTA)	2006
9 Trans-Pacific Strategic Economic Partnership (TPSEP)	2006	9 China–Singapore Free Trade Agreement (CSFTA)	2009
10 GCC–Singapore Free Trade Agreement (GSFTA)	2013	10 Peru–Singapore Free Trade Agreement (PeSFTA)	2009
11 EU–Singapore Free Trade Agreement (EUSFA)	signed Oct 2014	11 Singapore–Costa Rica Free Trade Agreement (SCRFTA)	2013
12 Comprehensive and Progressive TPP (CPTPP)	signed Feb 2016	12 Turkey–Singapore Free Trade Agreement (TRSFTA)	2017
13 Regional Comprehensive Economic Partnership (RCEP)	negotiating	13 Sri Lanka–Singapore Free Trade Agreement (SLSFTA)	2018

Source: Compiled by the author from database websites of Enterprise Singapore and the Asia Regional Integration Center of the Asian Development Bank.

Table 6.2: Most Favored Nation Tariffs on Nonagricultural Products
of Singapore's Free Trade Agreement Partners

FTA partners	Binding coverage %	Simple average bound rate %	Simple average applied rate %	Duty-free applied % coverage
ASEAN				
Brunei Darussalam	95.0	24.5	3.0	77.6
Indonesia	96.1	35.6	6.8	22.7
Malaysia	81.3	14.9	7.9	55.4
Philippines	61.8	23.4	5.8	3.1
Singapore	64.5	6.3	0.0	100.0
Thailand	70.9	25.5	8.2	20.6
Cambodia	100.0	17.7	13.7	5.6
Lao PDR	...	...	...	...
Myanmar	4.7	21.1	5.1	2.8
Viet Nam	100.0	10.4	15.7	35.6
Others				
Australia	96.5	11.0	3.9	45.6
Chile	100.0	25.0	6.0	0.3
PRC	100.0	9.1	9.0	7.3
India	69.8	34.9	16.4	2.4
Japan	99.6	2.7	2.8	55.1
Republic of Korea	93.8	10.1	6.6	15.9
New Zealand	99.9	10.4	3.2	62.1
Norway	100.0	3.1	0.6	94.2
Panama	100.0	22.9	6.4	36.3
Switzerland	99.7	2.6	2.1	18.7
United States	100.0	3.3	3.3	47.5

... = not available, ASEAN= Association of Southeast Asian Nations, FTA = free trade agreement, Lao PDR = Lao People's Democratic Republic, PRC= People's Republic of China.

Source: Chia, S.Y. 2011. Singapore. In M. Kawai and G. Wignaraja, eds. Asia's Free Trade Agreements: How is Business Responding? Cheltenham, UK, and Northampton, MA: Edward Elgar.

assembly and the final product is returned to Singapore for testing before export to the US and other destinations. The process rule recognizes outward processing, so both the value of parts and components made in Singapore as well as value of testing counts toward Singapore origin. This facilitates regional production networks and global supply chains. Under the Integrated Sourcing Initiative (ISI), certain products that are not made in Singapore, but exported through Singapore, are deemed of Singapore origin and entitled to preferential treatment when exported to the US. On textiles and garments, Singapore export into the US is subject to the "yarn forward" ROO, necessitating Singapore producers' change in sourcing in place of cheaper suppliers in East Asia.

Trade in services: The USSFTA adopts the "negative list" approach and provides for wide-ranging services trade liberalization. Singapore is committed to market access beyond the levels it committed in GATS. The market access provisions are supplemented by strong regulatory disciplines that also go beyond those mandated in GATS. The USSFTA also provides for mutual recognition of qualifications as well as certification and licensing requirements. Notable under the USSFTA is the opening of Singapore's financial services, telecommunication and e-commerce, and professional services to inroads from US service providers.

Other provisions: These include investment, intellectual property, competition and government enterprises, government procurement, temporary entry of business persons, and labor and environment.

6.2   ASEAN Economic Integration and Singapore's Position and Experiences

Overview

ASEAN is important to Singapore geopolitically and economically. On geopolitical considerations, Singapore is a small city-state in Southeast Asia and has to get on with its neighbors, particularly against the background of the Association of Southeast Asia, Maphilindo, Indonesian Konfrontasi, and the political split with Malaysia. On economic considerations, colonial Singapore has been the traditional entrepôt of Southeast Asia, but its intermediary role has never been easily understood and is often resented. This intermediation role became better understood with the growing literature on global and regional production networks and value chains. Independent Singapore needs a free global and regional trading environment to survive and prosper. It was the first Southeast Asian country to pursue export manufacturing in the 1960s and is thus heavily dependent on access to export markets. Also, it is heavily dependent on imports of capital goods, intermediate goods, natural resources and energy, as well as consumer goods.

The Singapore political leadership believes ASEAN economic cooperation should go hand in hand with geopolitical cooperation. As a highly open trade and FDI economy, Singapore would like ASEAN to be more open to trade and FDI. However, fully aware of the reservations and concerns of its bigger neighbors, Singapore has been treading softly in line with the comfort zone of others. Singapore supports ASEAN's concerns over commodities trade and over food and energy security. Singapore went along with the APTA, although it was a very inefficient way of trade liberalization. Singapore gave lukewarm support to the various ASEAN industrial cooperation schemes, although it does not subscribe to regional import substitution and an industrial policy of government "picking winners."

As one of ASEAN's founding fathers, Singapore's Foreign Minister Rajaratnam played a pivotal role in fostering ASEAN consensus and promoting a more cohesive and cooperative region. This consensual approach within ASEAN was marked by a willingness to recognize the concerns of other members. This often led ASEAN to adopt the lowest common denominator, or the "ASEAN Way." In its early years, there were divergent views among ASEAN member states on the role that ASEAN should play. Rajaratnam articulated Singapore's view that ASEAN was primarily an organization for promoting economic cooperation and not for resolving the region's military and security problems. However, this position changed markedly when Viet Nam invaded Cambodia in December 1978 and Rajaratnam gave strong support for ASEAN to become an important bulwark against the regional spread of communism.

Initial Obstacles to Economic Integration and Changed Rationale

ASEAN's preference for regional economic cooperation rather than integration in the 1970s and 1980s reflects the reluctance of some ASEAN members to undertake trade and investment liberalization due to the pursuit of import substitution and industrial policy of "picking winners." However, as the limitations of import substitution became increasingly apparent, more countries unilaterally adopted an outward-looking development strategy focusing on export orientation and foreign direct investment, thus paving the way for regional trade and investment liberalization.

Another obstacle to ASEAN economic integration at the time was the diversity in size, resource endowment, level of economic development, and technological capability among ASEAN member states, which led to differing perceptions of benefits and costs of economic integration. It was perceived that the more competitive ASEAN economies such as Singapore would gain more.[3] There were also political economy issues regarding the distribution of benefits and costs within each country. The winners from liberalization typically include consumers (the silent majority) who enjoy lower prices and wider range of goods and services; farmers, businesses, and workers in expanding export sectors; and foreign investors able to have right of establishment and a level playing field. The more vocal opposition includes uncompetitive farmers as well as businesses and workers in sectors threatened by import competition. With a change in emphasis toward the export market and attracting FDI and their production networks, ASEAN economic diversity became an integrating factor as differences in factor endowment and factor costs give rise to different comparative advantages to attract different segments of the global value chain. Singapore, in particular, played an important complementary role with its more technology- and knowledge-intensive exports and its regional services hub role.

Pre-ASEAN Free Trade Area Period, 1977–1992

In the 1970s and most of the 1980s, considerations of regional economic integration remained taboo in ASEAN and the focus was on economic cooperation. This period was characterized by preoccupation with cooperation on commodity trade problems, preferential market access under the APTA, and industrial cooperation schemes.

ASEAN Preferential Trading Arrangements
In July 1977, ASEAN ratified the Agreement on ASEAN Preferential Trading Arrangements, under which intra-ASEAN imports would enjoy a margin of preference on MFN tariffs. The APTA would cover 'basic commodities,' particularly food and energy, products of the industrial cooperation schemes, as well as other lists of goods to be negotiated. The product-by-

---

[3]   A regional redistributive mechanism would be unworkable as the most developed Singapore is only a city-state and the less developed Indonesia is an archipelagic nation with a huge population.

product negotiations initially covered only 71 items but reached 15,295 by 1990. The initial margin of preference of 10% was increased to 20%–25% in 1980 and the initial cutoff import value of $50,000 was abolished in 1984. Further, a 1987 protocol committed ASEAN members to place in the APTA within 5–7 years at least 90% of items traded among them with at least 50% of the value of intra-ASEAN trade; the margin of preference for the new items was raised to 25% and for those already in the APTA to 50%; the ASEAN content requirement was to be reduced in 5 years from 50% to 35%–42% and on a case-by-case basis after the 5 years.

As noted earlier, Singapore was less than enthusiastic over participation in the APTA. It had already dismantled most of its tariffs introduced during its "in Malaysia" period and had to hold back some tariffs for the APTA negotiations. Creative ways were adopted by ASEAN negotiators to increase the number of tariff lines available for negotiation, by splitting products into finer and finer categories.[4] There was obviously a lack of political will for ASEAN trade liberalization.

ASEAN Industrial Cooperation

During these early decades, ASEAN also dabbled in a number of industrial cooperation schemes: the 1976 ASEAN Industrial Projects (AIP), the 1981 ASEAN Industrial Complementation (AIC), and the 1983 ASEAN Industrial Joint Ventures (AIJV). Apparently this was influenced by the then prevailing regional import substitution and industrial policy of Latin American economic integration schemes.

The AIP program had a checkered history among the original five ASEAN members. ASEAN governments allocated five AIPs, with a urea fertilizer plant each for Indonesia and Malaysia, superphosphates for Philippines, diesel engines for Singapore, and soda ash for Thailand. The Basic Agreement on ASEAN Industrial Projects was signed in March 1980, containing the conditions for the projects: the host country would invest 60% of equity, while the other four ASEAN members would take the remaining 40% in equal shares. Of the five approved AIPs, only the urea fertilizer plants in Aceh (Indonesia) and Bintulu (Malaysia) survived as such; the other projects fell by the wayside for various reasons. For example, Singapore's diesel engine project met with difficulties as its

---

[4]   For example, a product like "matchboxes" could be split into multiple tariff lines by separate categorization of matchboxes according to the number of matchsticks they contain. Likewise, snowplows were introduced for negotiation, even though there was no demand in any ASEAN country.

ASEAN partners did not commit to providing market access because of competing domestic production. Singapore gave up the diesel engine project in favor of hepatitis B vaccines but failed to secure the necessary financing commitment from its ASEAN partners and so eventually withdrew its AIP proposal. Overall, the failure of the AIP scheme may be attributed to poor project identification and feasibility studies, financing problems, and conflicts between national industrial policies and attempts at regional industrial cooperation.

The AIC provided for allocation of "complementary" industrial products for manufacture by at least four ASEAN member states (or fewer if approved by ASEAN economic ministers). Products of AIC packages were to enjoy exclusive privileges: no AIC participant could manufacture the same product already allocated to another participant, with 2 years of exclusivity for existing products and 3 years for new products. Additionally, AIC products would qualify for preferences under the APTA with a 50% tariff margin of preference. Implementation problems arose from Malaysia's ambition to produce a Malaysian car and Singapore's reluctance to extend monopoly rights and protection for AIC products. In 1988, the AIC program was augmented with brand-to-brand (B-to-B) complementation specifically for the automotive industry: it provided a 50% margin of preference for specified parts and components of vehicles of a particular brand traded among approved ASEAN participants. Interested countries would negotiate individual packages for ASEAN approval. Malaysia, the Philippines, and Thailand were the initial participants, joined later by Indonesia. The first B-to-B complementation schemes were approved in 1989. In 1991, the B-to-B complementation scheme was expanded to cover non-automotive items as well, but by then the industrial complementation schemes were about to be superseded by AFTA and the ASEAN Industrial Cooperation (AICO) program.

To overcome the problem of requiring all ASEAN members to participate, under the 1983 AIJV program, projects needed equity participation of at least two member states to enjoy a 50% margin of preference for the first 4 years and market exclusivity for 3 years, provided they were "new" products, after which non-participating member states also had to extend the same margin of preference. In December 1987, a revised AIJV agreement enlarged the margin of preference to 90% and introduced more attractive equity schemes. However, difficulties arose from bureaucratic costs and confusions in regional and national legal applications. By 1991, enamel, heavy equipment, aluminum hydroxide, and Nestlé projects had been approved.

Assessment of Pre-ASEAN Free Trade Area Trade and Industrial Cooperation

The APTA was generally considered a failure, with considerable negotiating resources expended producing only a limited impact on intra-ASEAN trade. The 1991 ASEAN Economic Ministers' Meeting concluded that while intra-ASEAN trade in items covered by the APTA had grown from $121 million in 1987 to $578 million in 1989, it still accounted for an insignificant proportion of total intra-ASEAN trade.

What were the reasons for the APTA's failure? First, with tariff liberalization based on time-consuming product-by-product negotiations rather than across-the-board negotiations, and the prevalent import substituting industrialization policies, the lack of seriousness to liberalize intra-ASEAN trade was highlighted by the inclusion of snowplows and nuclear plants in the negotiations and the long national exclusion lists. Second, a 1986 study by the United Nations Industrial Development Organization highlighted underlying structural difficulties and institutional biases. Existing trade and production patterns had allowed only limited absorptive capacity in the ASEAN member states for each other's major commodity exports which were primarily destined for extra-ASEAN demand; and import substituting industrialization policies and balance-of-payments difficulties faced by some ASEAN members had resulted in an import structure dominated by capital and intermediate goods sourced from developed countries.

The various industrial cooperation schemes aimed at regional import substitution failed in ASEAN as they did in Latin America. ASEAN member states were engaged in industrial policies of import substitution and building national champions resulting in conflicting national interests. The schemes highlighted national differences and did not contribute significantly to industrial development of the countries (except for B-to-B complementation in the automotive sector and Nestlé's multi-country plants).

ASEAN Free Trade Area Period, 1992–2002

Through the 1980s, ASEAN member states (other than Singapore) were unilaterally abandoning import substitution in favor of export manufacturing. From the late 1980s, dramatic global and regional developments were pressuring ASEAN to move toward regional economic integration so as to compete effectively for global markets and investments. The Uruguay Round was completed in December 1991 and GATT was being reorganized into the WTO; the EU was being created by the Treaty of Maastricht in February 1992; NAFTA was being negotiated; and radical economic reforms were taking place in the PRC, followed by India.

ASEAN Free Trade Area, ASEAN Framework Agreement on Services, ASEAN Investment Area, and ASEAN Industrial Cooperation

Proposals from a number of ASEAN member states on economic integration included the Common Effective Preferential Tariff (CEPT) scheme favored by the Philippines and the ASEAN Free Trade Area favored by Thailand and Singapore. The Fourth ASEAN Summit in Singapore in 1992 approved the AFTA initiative and Singapore Prime Minister Goh Chok Tong declared:

> "Unless ASEAN can match the other regions in attractiveness both as a base for investments as well as a market for their products, investments by MNCs are likely to flow away from our part of the world to the Single European Market and NAFTA. If we do not synergize our strengths, ASEAN will risk missing the boat" (Severino 2006: 224).

ASEAN agreed to establish AFTA in January 1992 and the agreement entered into force in January 1993, with intra-ASEAN tariff liberalization under the CEPT scheme. A customs union with common external tariffs was ruled out in view of the marked differences in MFN tariff levels among ASEAN economies, particularly between Singapore and the rest. The original agreement was to reduce tariffs to the 0%–5% level over a 15-year period. Since then, all tariffs in the CEPT Inclusion List were to be eliminated by ASEAN-6 (Brunei Darussalam, Indonesia, Malaysia, the Philippines, Singapore, and Thailand) by 2010 and by Cambodia, the Lao People's Democratic Republic (Lao PDR), Myanmar, and Viet Nam (CLMV) by 2015.

By the early 1990s, economic integration elsewhere in the world (e.g., NAFTA) had moved beyond traditional free trade in goods to encompass services and investments. Hence, AFTA was complemented by the 1995 ASEAN Framework Agreement on Services (AFAS) and by the 1998 Framework Agreement on the ASEAN Investment Area (AIA). AFAS requires negotiations to be conducted sector by sector, with each round of negotiations resulting in a package of commitments in each agreed sector and/or subsector and mode of supply. By August 2018, member states have negotiated and agreed on 10 packages of commitments under AFAS. These cover business services, professional services, construction, distribution, education, environmental services, health care, maritime transport, telecommunication, and tourism. ASEAN has also concluded mutual recognition arrangements or mutual recognition arrangement frameworks for professional services covering engineering, architecture, accountancy, surveying, medical practitioners, dental practitioners, nursing services, and tourism professionals. However, services liberalization under AFAS has not kept pace with goods liberalization under AFTA. The Mid-Term Review of the Ha Noi Plan of Action suggested that there were still substantial barriers to integration in services. Many negotiators are extremely cautious, either because of their uncertainty about the impact of liberalization and fear of the loss of regulatory control in some service sectors (such as financial services) or because of the power of domestic interests.

In the AIA, sector coverage includes manufacturing, agriculture, fisheries, forestry and mining, and services incidental to these sectors. ASEAN-6 and Myanmar agreed to phase out their temporary exclusion lists (TELs) in manufacturing by 2003; and Cambodia, the Lao PDR, and Viet Nam by 2010. Malaysia and Singapore did not have TELs. According to the Mid-Term Review of the Ha Noi Plan of Action, some countries faced difficulties in drawing up their TEL and sensitive list for services that are incidental to manufacturing, agriculture, fishery, forestry, and mining, and submissions were delayed until 2002. The extent and type of barriers to investment are indicated by the length and content of these TELs, sensitive lists, and general exclusion lists. In 2003, the sector coverage was expanded to include education, health care, telecommunication, tourism, banking and finance, insurance, trading, e-commerce, distribution and logistics, transportation and warehousing, and professional services such as accounting, engineering, and advertising. The deadlines for phasing out the TELs ranged from January 2003 to 2015, depending on country and sector. The general exclusion lists consists of industries and investment measures that are not open to FDI for reasons of national security, public morals, public health, and environmental protection. As with services liberalization, the "ASEAN Minus X" formula was introduced.

To improve the investment climate, the AIA Agreement calls for the reduction and/or elimination of regulations and conditions impeding investment flows and investment project operation. Also, ASEAN members are to exchange their action plans on facilitating, promoting, and liberalizing inflows of investments, with the ASEAN Secretariat tasked to compile and publish the plans. The AIA also contains an investment promotion program, which includes joint investment promotion missions to target countries, creation of investment websites and databases, and timely publication of investment information. Reports are that the joint investment promotion missions failed in their objective of attracting FDI into ASEAN as a destination, as national investment agencies focused on attracting FDI into their own respective territories.

In 1996, ASEAN also adopted a new industrial cooperation scheme to replace earlier industrial cooperation schemes. The objective of AICO is to promote joint manufacturing between ASEAN-based companies. The qualifying criteria for AICO are a minimum of two companies in two different member states and a minimum of 30% national equity. Unlike the earlier schemes, in which ASEAN members collectively decided on product coverage, AICO allows the private sector to select the products for which to seek tariff concessions, subject to approval of AICO status by the governments immediately involved. Also unlike earlier schemes where products enjoy exclusivity but not necessarily enjoy low tariffs, AICO products do not enjoy exclusivity but immediately enjoy AFTA end-tariff rates of 0%–5% as well as local content accreditation and investment incentives offered by ASEAN national authorities. With tariff levels for intra-ASEAN-6 trade reaching the 0%–5% level by 2002, the AICO scheme was amended so that all AICO-eligible products enjoy zero tariffs. Most of the AICO applicants are in the electronics and automotive sectors and involve well-known companies in these sectors. Only Indonesia, Malaysia, the Philippines, and Thailand have participated extensively in AICO; Singapore and Viet Nam are each involved in only three projects with two in electronics and one in automotive components. AICO has successfully promoted production networks in the automobile and electronics industries.

Assessment of Economic Integration during the ASEAN Free Trade Area Period

A common yardstick to measure the extent of economic integration achieved is to look at progress in intra-regional trade. Intra-ASEAN trade share has grown from 17.0% in 1990 (pre-AFTA) to 25.0% in recent years, representing a significant improvement. Critics point out that this trade share is still significantly lower than that achieved by regional groupings such as NAFTA and the EU. Further, the improved trade share may not necessarily be attributable to the implementation of AFTA, particularly as business utilization rates of CEPT tariff preferences were low. It could be counterargued that the raison d'être of ASEAN economic integration (as ascertained from various statements issued at Summit and ministerial meetings and from comments of various ASEAN leaders and officials) is not intra-ASEAN trade but improving ASEAN's competitiveness in attracting FDI and exports—and this is particularly Singapore's perspective. A constant trade share shows that intra-ASEAN trade has been growing *pari passu* with ASEAN's global trade. However, ASEAN's share of global FDI destined for the developing world has been declining in recent decades, mainly attributable to the rise of the PRC as an investment destination as well as the impact of the Asian Financial Crisis on ASEAN's investment climate. Intra-ASEAN investments have been growing rapidly.

The 2001 Mid-Term Review of the Ha Noi Plan of Action highlighted some of the implementation problems during the AFTA period. First, weak commitments to some of the decisions to promote liberalization and cooperation programs, possibly due to poor awareness of the benefits of liberalization. Weak commitment was also reflected in the low level of representation at negotiations and meetings, resulting in the inability to make critical decisions at such meetings. Second, slowness in implementing decisions that have been taken, due to the need to consider the interests of all stakeholders at the national level, particularly when there are perceived conflicts between regional commitments and national and/or sector interests. Third, legislative changes to ratify agreements and commitments could be time-consuming. Fourth, implementation delays may be due to lack of appropriate and sufficient technical capacity for implementation. Fifth, some of the activities of ASEAN need to involve the private sector and such consultations have to be initiated. Sixth, there were inadequate financial resources to support ASEAN's programs.

ASEAN Economic Community Period, 2003–2015

The Rationale for the ASEAN Economic Community
At the November 2002 ASEAN Summit, it was decided to move on to the next stage of regional economic integration. The main rationale for the AEC was weakened ability of ASEAN to attract FDI in the aftermath of the Asian Financial Crisis and the economic rise of the PRC and India. For ASEAN to meet these challenges, it would have to deepen economic integration to persuade investors that an integrated ASEAN would also have a sizable market and production base to compete with the PRC. The AEC was created at the Bali Summit in 2003. It has four major pillars and objectives: single market and production base, competitive economic region, equitable economic development, and integration into the global economy. In April 2009, the completion date of the AEC was advanced from 2020 to 2015.

ASEAN Economic Community Blueprint and Its Implementation

The AEC Blueprint, adopted in November 2007, outlines the various strategic measures and time schedules for implementation during the 2008–2015 period.

The AEC Scorecard 2012 (ASEAN Secretariat 2012) tracks the implementation, gaps, and challenges of the various measures and strategic schedules in the AEC Blueprint. For 2008–2011, the implementation rate was 65.9% for the single market and production base, 67.9% for the competitive economic region, 66.7% for equitable economic development, and 85.7% for integration into the global economy. The AEC Scorecard only records compliance or noncompliance with the measures in the ASEAN capital cities (as it would be difficult to monitor implementation in the outlying provinces and islands of ASEAN's bigger countries). It gives no indication whether implementation is adequate to achieve the AEC declared objectives by 2015. In the typical "ASEAN Way" there are no penalties for noncompliance or efforts to "name and shame."

In 2012, two lists of Prioritized Key Deliverables (PKDs) were drawn for implementation by 2013 and by 2015 to prioritize areas in which implementation would be critical to the AEC. ASEAN reviewed the unimplemented PKDs in 2015 and more prioritization took place. Among the unimplemented PKDs, 54 measures (called high-priority measures or HPMs) were identified to have the greatest impact on trade and could be realistically implemented by end-2015. These 54 HPMs, together with 452 measures already fully implemented since 2008, formed a more focused base of 506 measures for monitoring implementation, giving an implementation rate of 92.7% as of end-October 2015. But based on the total 611 AEC measures, the implementation rate was only 79.5% (Chia 2016).

Shortfalls in the AEC Blueprint implementation are often attributed to "lack of political will" and conflicting interests of different stakeholders. In any trade and investment liberalization initiative, there are winners and losers. Policy makers have the tough task of marketing the liberalization idea, seeking consultations with various stakeholders to identify short-term losers, and finding mechanisms to "compensate" them through financial, technical, and job training assistance to enable firms to seek new businesses and workers to find new jobs. Some ASEAN member states, including Singapore, have been more successful than others in achieving this objective. Also, it would not be unreasonable to assume that Singapore is not a laggard implementer, since it has already undertaken extensive trade in goods, trade in services, and foreign investment liberalization unilaterally and under several bilateral FTAs.

At the 24th ASEAN Summit in Nay Pyi Taw in May 2014, the Nay Pyi Taw Declaration on Realisation of the ASEAN Community by 2015 was adopted, providing policy guidance to ensure the successful establishment of the ASEAN Community by 2015.

In late November 2015, the ASEAN Secretariat released two documents outlining progress toward the AEC's objectives of a single market and production base, competitive economic region, equitable economic development, and integration into the global economy.[5] The AEC came into being on 31 December 2015. There was no "big bang" as many of the measures and actions have been progressively implemented over the years. The most noticeable effect by end-2015 was tariff elimination. Most AEC Blueprint measures have not been fully implemented. Nontariff barrier elimination is problematic, since many nontariff measures also serve regulatory purposes. Trade facilitation measures are not completed, including improvement of customs procedures, ASEAN Single Window, and e-commerce. FDI liberalization and facilitation remains a "work in progress." So are measures for harmonization of standards, intellectual property rights, competition policy, SME development, capital market development, and transport and logistics development.

AEC 2025 Blueprint—Forging Ahead Together
The AEC 2025 builds on the 4 pillars of the AEC 2015, with emphasis on integration areas that are still "works in progress" as well as "future-looking." Economists who expected that ASEAN would progress toward a customs union or a common market were disappointed as the AEC 2025 remains very much a continuation of the AEC 2015. The AEC 2025 is envisioned to:

(i) create a deeply integrated and highly cohesive ASEAN economy to support sustained high economic growth and resilience ;
(ii) engender a more equitable and inclusive economic growth in ASEAN that narrows the development gap and significantly reduces or eliminates poverty;

---

5   ASEAN Secretariat 2015a. A Blueprint for Growth: ASEAN Economic Community 2015: Progress and Key Achievements; and ASEAN Secretariat 2015b. ASEAN Integration Report 2015.

(iii) foster robust productivity growth through innovation, technology and human resource development to increase ASEAN's competitive edge in moving up the global value chain into higher technology and knowledge-intensive manufacturing and service industries;

(iv) promote good governance, transparency, and responsive regulatory regimes through active engagements with the private sector and other ASEAN stakeholders;

(v) widen ASEAN people-to-people, institutional, and infrastructure connectivity through ASEAN and sub-regional cooperation projects that facilitate movement of capital as well as skilled labour and talents; and

(vi) create a more dynamic and resilient ASEAN to respond and adjust to emerging challenges.

Why is ASEAN not a Customs Union?

The idea of an ASEAN Customs Union surfaces from time to time. In the world of economic integration, there have been few customs unions and plenty of FTAs; a customs union requires substantial surrender of national sovereignty. ASEAN as a customs union could have an advantage over the current AEC (with features of FTAs and some elements of single market) in that there will be a common external tariff that obviates the need for ROOs to prevent trade deflection. Singapore is usually identified as the obstacle to ASEAN progressing toward a customs union because of its zero tariff position. ASEAN as a customs union would require Singapore as well as low-tariff countries to raise tariffs (which usually corresponds to a grouping's median level); this would be disastrous for Singapore's free port status and contravene the WTO requirement that an FTA or customs union not raise trade barriers against nonmembers and thus invite penalties and retaliation. To the extent that ASEAN member states would multilateralize their CEPT concessions, it would result in a convergence of ASEAN MFN tariff levels ultimately to zero, and also minimize the trade diversion effects of AFTA and the ASEAN Trade in Goods Agreement. For some ASEAN economies, the issue of loss of tariff revenue is an important consideration. Additionally, a customs union would require pooling of other commercial policies, including the role of state-owned enterprises, resulting in some loss of policy space and national sovereignty, which would be unpalatable to some ASEAN members.

6.3   Conclusion

In Retrospect

ASEAN economic cooperation and integration have come a long way. From a set of token cooperative initiatives during its first few decades to the current AEC, ASEAN has made serious efforts at deepening economic integration in the region. This is now complemented by intensified efforts at realizing ASEAN connectivity. Outward orientation and "open regionalism" have served ASEAN well. It has been one of the fastest growing regions in the world in recent decades. It is a work in progress toward the AEC 2025. Improved and more transparent mechanisms of monitoring have been put in place to ensure a better compliance record for the AEC 2025. Integration should be viewed as an ongoing process, driven by market forces and regional production networks and buttressed and facilitated by formal AEC measures.

Narrowing the Development Gap in ASEAN
More socially equitable and environmentally sustainable growth is now the mantra driving international and regional organizations such as the World Bank and the Asian Development Bank as well as many national development agendas. How is ASEAN going to meet the challenge of its wide development gap intracountry and intracountry? ASEAN member states, since the accession of CLMV in the 1990s, have been faced with a development divide between the original ASEAN-6 and the newer CLMV members and plugging that gap is one of the declared objectives of the AEC. By various economic growth, per capita income, and human development criteria, the gap has narrowed between the two subgroups, particularly between middle-income ASEAN and Viet Nam. Nevertheless, much more needs to be done. There have been proposals for ASEAN to adopt EU-style structural funds but their adoption in ASEAN faces severe difficulties: issues of defining which subregions of ASEAN (not countries) require structural fund support, what should be the funding mechanism, and how to bring various ASEAN stakeholders on board to support the idea. Ultimately, accelerating a country's economic growth and development will depend a great deal on the country itself. ASEAN can best help by providing regional public goods such as an environment of geopolitical, social, and financial stability; improving ASEAN connectivity and logistics; and mitigating the negative impacts of natural disasters and pandemics. The more developed ASEAN member states can offer cooperation in areas such as agricultural and rural development, technological development and technology

transfer, public sector management, and SME development. The CLMV countries will have to ensure a favorable business and investment climate to attract more FDI from within ASEAN and the richer ASEAN economies would need to respond with more financial and technical assistance and private sector investment. Singapore has been playing an active role in this regard—it is the largest source of intra-ASEAN official financial and technical assistance and largest source of intra-ASEAN investment by government and private enterprises.

Wider Asian Economic Integration beyond ASEAN?

Widening economic integration beyond ASEAN is in Singapore's economic interest, especially since it already has bilateral FTAs with economies all over the world and multilateralism in the WTO appears to be in limbo. It also facilitates Singapore's role in the global and regional value chain.

ASEAN and individual ASEAN member states are also pursuing ASEAN Plus FTAs. ASEAN has been proactive in establishing economic integration agreements with (ASEAN+1 FTAs) with the PRC, Japan, the Republic of Korea, India, and Australia–New Zealand. And in the ASEAN Summit of November 2011, it launched the Regional Comprehensive Economic Partnership (RCEP) initiative. Negotiations on RCEP began in early 2013. It remains to be seen whether the RCEP will become a reality. It also remains to be seen whether "ASEAN centrality" can be maintained.

References

ASEAN Secretariat. 2012. *ASEAN Economic Community Scorecard.* March 2012. Jakarta.

ASEAN Secretariat. 2015a. *A Blueprint for Growth: ASEAN Economic Community 2015: Progress and Key Achievements.* Jakarta: ASEAN Secretariat.

ASEAN Secretariat. 2015b. *ASEAN Integration Report 2015.* Jakarta: ASEAN Secretariat.

ASEAN Secretariat. 2015c. *ASEAN 2025: Forging Ahead Together.* Jakarta: ASEAN Secretariat.

ASEAN Secretariat. www.asean.org/asean/asean-secretariat.

Asian Development Bank. 2015. Asia Regional Integration Center. https://aric.adb.org.

Chia, S.Y. 2011. Singapore. In M. Kawai and G. Wignaraja, eds. *Asia's Free Trade Agreements: How is Business Responding?* Cheltenham, UK and Northampton, MA: Edward Elgar.

Chia, S.Y. 2016. Modalities for ASEAN Economic Integration: Retrospect and Going Forward. *The Singapore Economic Review* 62 (03): 561-591.

Desker, B. and M.N.M. Osman. 2006. S. Rajaratnam and the Making of Singapore Foreign Policy. In Kwa Chong Guan, ed. *S Rajaratnam on Singapore: From Ideas to Reality.* Singapore: Institute of Southeast Asian Studies.

Enterprise Singapore. 2018. Free Trade Agreements (FTAs). https://www.enterprisesg.gov.sg/non-financial-assistance/for-singapore-companies/free-trade-agreements/ftas/overview.

Severino, R. 2006. *Southeast Asia in Search of an ASEAN Community: Insights from the Former ASEAN Secretary-General.* Singapore: Institute of Southeast Asian Studies/Asian Development Bank.

World Trade Organization. Trade Policy Review: Singapore (2012). https://www.wto.org/english/tratop_e/tpr_e/tp367_e.htm.

Launching the ASEAN Community. At the 27th ASEAN Summit held in Malaysia in November 2015, ASEAN Leaders announced the establishment of the ASEAN Community on 31 December 2015 (photos from the ASEAN Secretariat Photo Archives).

CHAPTER 7
ASEAN ECONOMIC COMMUNITY: MALAYSIA'S EVOLVING PERSPECTIVES

Tham Siew Yean

This chapter examines how national interests have influenced Malaysia's priorities for ASEAN cooperation and its implementation of ASEAN agreements. The chapter also discusses current trade and investment issues.

Introduction

The search for growth is part of the quest for economic prosperity that is aspired for by both developed and developing nations. It is especially essential for Malaysia where poverty reduction as well as the redistribution of wealth among the ethnic groups, from the non-Bumiputeras to the Bumiputeras (or the Malays and other indigenous groups in the country) is of paramount importance. These twin goals were encapsulated in the New Economic Policy (NEP) that was launched in 1971 in response to the interethnic riots in 1969. Economic growth is a fundamental condition for achieving the goals of the NEP. Moreover, the country has also targeted developed country status by 2020 based on Vision 2020 that was put forward by Prime Minister Mahathir Mohamad.

The need for growth, poverty reduction, and income redistribution has led to extensive state interventions in the economic development of the country. In the case of growth, state intervention was used to facilitate the shift from primary commodity to manufacturing production to engineer the necessary economic transformation from a traditional agro-based economy to an industrial-based economy. For example, the use of a foreign direct investment-led model for developing the manufacturing sector was facilitated through investment promotion and investment incentives as well as the development of specific institutions such as free trade zones.

The need for growth has become more urgent since recovering from the Asian financial crisis (AFC) in 1997–1998 as the growth rate of the country has almost halved since then. Moreover in 2010, then Prime Minister Najib Razak set forth a new target of achieving a high-income economy by

2020, with per capita income of $15,000 (Government of Malaysia 2010). This would entail for income per capita of the country to more than double in slightly less than a decade from $6,760 in 2009. This will require Malaysia to achieve an average annual real growth rate of 6% between 2011 and 2020 for it to realize its high-income objective.

While growth demands a more liberalized economy, affirmative action demands otherwise. How can Malaysia balance these two conflicting needs? Specifically, in the case of the Association of Southeast Asian Nations (ASEAN), are there any changes in Malaysia's perspectives on economic liberalization and cooperation over time? This chapter seeks to analyze these changes from the time ASEAN was formed until now. It also examines the possible future direction for ASEAN economic integration from Malaysia's perspective, given the historical pattern of its participation in ASEAN economic cooperation and liberalization efforts.

7.1   Original Motivation and Vision

Malaysia, as in the case of other older ASEAN member states, was originally politically motivated to join ASEAN in 1967 for the preservation of peace and to balance the roles of outside powers (Buzynski 1998). Malaysia's first prime minister, Tunku Abdul Rahman, was initially reluctant as he preferred to expand the Association of Southeast Asia (ASA), which was the forerunner of ASEAN. However, he was persuaded by Thailand to join ASEAN. Moreover, he was also advised by ministry officials that Malaysia should not stay aloof from trends in Southeast Asia and that Indonesia's membership would benefit Malaysia and the region (Fitfield 1979). This is reflected in the speech of then Deputy Prime Minister Tun Abdul Razak, who signed the Bangkok Declaration on the founding of ASEAN in 1967. In his speech, he noted that the countries of Southeast Asia should be willing to take responsibility for their own destiny. He conjured a vision of an ASEAN that would include all the countries of Southeast Asia and further "stressed that the countries of the region should recognize that unless they assumed their common responsibility to shape their own destiny and to prevent external intervention and interference, Southeast Asia would remain fraught with danger and tension. And unless they took decisive and collective action to prevent the eruption of intra-regional conflicts, the nations of Southeast Asia would remain susceptible to manipulation, one against another" (ASEAN Secretariat, undated, www.asean.org/asean/about-asean/history).

While the constitution of ASEAN in 1967 included economic rationales, the seeds for economic cooperation were sown through the numerous bilateral meetings that were held from 1967 to 1976. Economic cooperation was, however, confined to a mixture of sector and commodity-based concerns under the ASEAN Foreign Ministers' Meeting in the initial organizational structure of ASEAN after the Bangkok Declaration (ASEAN Secretariat 1997). It was almost a decade later that the first economic ministerial meeting took place at the 1976 Bali Summit, prompted in part by the 1973–1975 recession in the United Kingdom and the United States (US).

7.2   Changes in Perspectives over Time

Pre-ASEAN Free Trade Area

ASEAN's approach toward economic cooperation was both cautious and slow due to the "ASEAN Way." Initial attempts focused on selective economic integration in industry and trade with the signing of the ASEAN Industrial Projects (AIP) in 1976 and the Agreement on ASEAN Preferential Trading Arrangements (APTA) in 1977. Several other attempts at industrial cooperation were launched subsequently, such as the ASEAN Industrial Complementation (AIC) scheme in 1981 (subsequently modified as the ASEAN Brand-to-Brand Complementation) and the ASEAN Industrial Joint Ventures (AIJV) in 1983.

This cautious approach suited Malaysia's own approach toward economic cooperation, as its participation in economic cooperation within ASEAN was dictated by its national interests. This can be seen clearly in the instances when Malaysia participated in cooperation and when it was reluctant to lend support to ASEAN economic initiatives. In the case of the former, Malaysia had embarked on industrialization through import substitution after independence. It had switched to export promotion in the late 1960s and used free trade zones in the early 1970s to industrialize. Since the urea AIP project was already slated as a national project, Malaysia was able to implement the project unlike other projects in the AIP scheme which did not take off due to various reasons, including lack of private sector interest and inadequate financial and technical support (Kurus 1993; Ravenhill 1995). In the case of the APTA, Malaysia—as in the case of Indonesia and the Philippines—was also reluctant to open up its markets, leading to the dismal failure of the trade liberalization scheme, where trade in 16,000 products that nominally enjoyed preferences under the APTA amounted to less than 1% of intra-ASEAN trade (Ravenhill 1995).

However, the Malaysian economy plunged into its first economic recession after independence in 1985 (Table 7.1) due to the congruence of adverse internal and external conditions. Externally, the economic downturn in developed countries triggered by the US high interest rate policy in the early 1980s resulted in a massive collapse of world commodity trade (Athukorala 2012). Between 1984 and 1986, Malaysia's overall export price index declined by 30%, reflecting a sharp decline in tin and palm oil prices while the terms of trade deteriorated by almost 20% in these years. Internally, Malaysia suffered from twin deficits. Its fiscal deficit ballooned due to the implementation of the heavy industries project, which required huge capital outlays. At the same time, its trade deficit also widened with the import of capital and intermediate goods needed by the heavy industries that were far from ready to compete in the export market. The economy contracted by 10% in 1985 and lasted for 1 year. Consequently, Malaysia embarked on domestic liberalization in its foreign direct investment (FDI) policy to attract FDI into the country. This included three significant changes. First, the investment threshold used for the application of the Industrial Coordination Act that was promulgated in 1975 to meet the restructuring targets of the NEP was increased from $400,000 to approximately $1 million or more (or to plants employing more than 75 workers). Second, foreign investors could own 100% of new projects, subject to export conditions, and restrictions on the number of expatriate workers employed in foreign affiliates were eased also. Third, the Promotions of Investment Act (1986) was introduced to replace the Investment Incentive Act (1968) with attractive incentives provided for foreign investors.

These policy changes coincided with the surge in outward FDI from the newly industrialized economies (NIEs), especially from Japan due to the appreciation of the yen against the dollar following the Plaza Accord. Malaysia rapidly became a popular host economy for such outward FDI owing to the changes in its investment policies, as well as other attractive host country advantages such as relatively low wages, political stability, and good infrastructure facilities. From the mid-1980s to the onset of the AFC, FDI flows had been increasing at a faster rate than flows to all other ASEAN economies (Menon 2014). FDI flows increased more than tenfold to reach $4 billion from 1987 to 1991. This prompted Malaysia to industrialize by joining global value chains especially in the electronics sector, which in turn contributed to the increase in exports of manufactured goods, again especially in electronics.

Real gross domestic product (GDP) grew at an average of 6.9% from 1986 to 1990, while the real GDP growth rate averaged 9.5% from 1991 to 1995 (Table 7.1). The 10 long years of robust growth enabled Malaysia to transform its economic structure from a primary commodity to manufacturing producer. Specifically, the share of manufacturing in GDP doubled from 13.9% in 1970 to 26.4% in 1995. Malaysia, like the other older ASEAN member states, was then touted to join the ranks of the NIEs and thus became confident that its domestic industries would be able to withstand the pressures of trade liberalization. Thus, it joined the other member states to commit to tariff liberalization under the Common Effective Preferential Tariff (CEPT) scheme in 1992.

Table 7.1: Real Gross Domestic Product Growth Rates, 1971–2017 (%)

Year	1971– 1975	1976– 1980	1981– 1985	1986– 1990	1991– 1995	1996– 2000	2001– 2005	2006– 2010	2011– 2015	2016– 2017
Year 1	10.0	11.6	7.0	1.2	9.6	10.0	0.5	5.6	5.3	4.2
Year 2	9.4	7.8	6.0	5.4	8.9	7.3	5.4	6.3	5.5	5.9
Year 3	11.7	6.7	6.2	10.0	9.9	−7.4	5.8	4.8	4.7	n.a.
Year 4	8.3	9.3	7.8	9.1	9.2	6.1	6.8	−1.5	6.0	n.a.
Year 5	0.8	7.4	−1.1	9.0	9.8	8.9	5.3	7.4	5.0	n.a.
Average	8.0	8.6	5.2	6.9	9.5	5.0	4.8	4.5	5.3	5.1

n.a. = not available.
Source: Department of Statistics, Malaysia. Time Series Data. https://www.dosm.gov.my/v1/index.php?r=column/ctimeseries&menu_id=NHJlaGc2Rlg4ZXlGTjh1SU1kaWY5UT09 (accessed 16 August 2018); and The Performance of State's Economy, 2017. https://www.dosm.gov.my/v1/index.php?r=column/cthemeByCat&cat=449&bul_id=L25EUXQxbWdBaEVoWXU5aTFQWUpNdz09&menu_id=TE5CRUZCblh4ZTZMODZlbmk2aWRRQT09 (accessed 16 August 2018).

ASEAN Free Trade Area and Malaysia's Development Needs

The implementation of the AFTA commitments was problematic for Malaysia, especially for its automotive sector. Malaysia had initiated its national car project as part of the country's heavy industries development that was launched in 1980. The government established a national car, Proton, in 1983 with Mitsubishi as its foreign partner. Proton was protected from the start with tariffs as well as nontariff measures, resulting in a significant price difference compared to non-national cars. This enabled the national car to capture a large share of Malaysia's automotive sector, reaching 74% by 1993. A second national car was established that year (Perodua) to manufacture subcompact cars with Daihatsu from Japan. Both focused on producing for the protected domestic market rather than exporting. Moreover, the need to lend support to the Vendor Development Programme—designed to facilitate the development of Bumiputera entrepreneurs in the automotive sector—affected the cost-competitiveness of Proton. The vendors that serviced Proton alone lacked economies of scale unlike more outward-looking vendors.

The onset of the AFC in 1997 caused a sharp fall in Malaysian automotive production and domestic sales. Malaysia reverted back to protectionist policies for its automotive sector, leading to the exclusion of its automotive sector from AFTA liberalization schedules beyond its 2003 deadline (Tham 2004). Subsequently, tariffs on automotive products were reduced to 20% in 2005 and scrapped in 2010. The reduction in tariffs was offset by an increase in excise duties, purportedly to compensate for the loss in tariff revenues. These excise duties could be lowered by meeting the requirements of the Industrial Linkage Programme to increase local value-added activities. Excise duties ranged between 65% and 105%, with an average of 50%. For Proton, its net excise duty was less than 10%, because it had reportedly attained 90% local value-added activities. Consequently, a two-tier market existed in Malaysia's automotive sector: one for national cars and another for non-national cars. In 2012, Proton was sold by Khazanah Nasional Berhad, Malaysia's sovereign wealth fund, to a private Bumiputera company, DRB-HICOM Berhad. Despite the change in Proton's ownership status to a private company, it continues to receive preferential treatment. In 2014, the Land Public Transport Commission issued a mandate for all budget and executive taxi operators to change their cars to a brown Proton Exora when their permits expired by 31 October 2014 (The Star Online 2014).

Similarly, Malaysia was also hesitant to grant approvals for the ASEAN Industrial Cooperation (AICO) scheme, which was created in 1996 to serve as an early harvest of AFTA. Companies operating in two or more ASEAN member states could qualify for the early application of the 0%–5% AFTA rates for their production inputs and finished goods if they could demonstrate that resource sharing and/or industrial complementation was involved in their projects. Objections were raised on the basis that these programs benefited foreign multinational corporations rather than indigenous enterprises. However, the reduction of tariffs for foreign-affiliated firms based on AICO privileges would have meant cost savings for these firms and conversely an erosion of the tariff protection gains for national cars (Yoshimutsu 2002).[1]

Malaysia's concern over development needs has also influenced its stance in the ASEAN Investment Area (AIA) that was launched in 1995 to counter the large inflows of FDI that were drawn to the emerging large market in the People's Republic of China (PRC). The AIA therefore sought to encourage inflows of FDI into ASEAN by offering economies of scale through an enlarged ASEAN market generated by regional economic integration and intra-ASEAN investment liberalization. According to Nesadurai (2003), however, Malaysia advocated a developmental role for the AIA to reduce its dependence on FDI and to nurture domestic capital. Malaysia thus favored preferential treatment for ASEAN investors for 10 years over non-ASEAN investors—for nurturing domestic capital to become ASEAN conglomerates. It viewed a crucial part of the AIA as encouraging the development of ASEAN conglomerates through joint ventures or other alliances between ASEAN investors as a means of competing with the global corporate giants. As explained by a senior official from the ASEAN Secretariat, "the ASEAN countries saw the need to develop ASEAN multinationals using the grace period before foreign (non-ASEAN) investors would be accorded the same privileges" (Nesadurai 2003: 113). However, the impact of the AIA on intra-ASEAN investment was not significant due to its problematic implementation, including among others, tacit investment protectionism through reclassification and redesignation of sectors from temporary exclusion lists to sensitive lists, stringent conditionality clauses, and a default investment screening system (Masron and Yusop 2012; Jarvis 2012).

Affirmative actions also affected the liberalization of services as government-linked companies (GLCs) were prevalent in this sector due to the privatization and corporatization of the legacy monopolies that prevailed in this sector.[2] GLCs have to support the Vendor Development Programme for Bumiputeras as well as preferential procurement from Bumiputera companies. Although the ASEAN Framework Agreement on Services (AFAS) was also signed in 1995, progress in liberalization of services was slow as services in most ASEAN member states, including Malaysia, are inward oriented.

---

[1]   Malaysia did eventually approve complementation projects in the AICO scheme, and automotive firms in the country participated in about half of all automotive-related projects in this program. These projects involved mainly Japanese firms with only one involving Perodua and none for Proton (Postigo 2013).

[2]   GLCs are defined as companies in which the government owns at least 20% of the issued and paid-up capital.

Post-ASEAN Free Trade Area

ASEAN Economic Community

The launch of the ASEAN Economic Community (AEC) in 2003 came at a period when Malaysia's high growth rates had faltered after the AFC. The average growth rate for 1996–2000 was 4.8% and averaged 3.9% for 2001–2003, contributed in part by the dot-com crisis in 2001 (Table 7.1). More importantly, Malaysia was losing its draw as an investment destination due to rising labor costs at home as well as increasing attractiveness of other host economies, including the PRC. This was further exacerbated by the global slowdown in FDI flows, which declined by more than half from $134 billion in 2000 to $63 billion in 2003 (Menon 2014). Unlike other crisis-affected countries, FDI flows into Malaysia did not bounce back after the economic recovery in 1999 and Malaysia lost its position as the second largest recipient of FDI flows to Thailand in 2000. The importance of FDI to Malaysia's economy can be seen in its contribution to the growth of manufacturing output, employment and exports, as well as technological spillovers that facilitate the acquisition of the requisite technology needed to move up the value-added chain of production (see, e.g., Bende-Nabebde 2001; Marwah and Tavakoli 2004). Malaysia's aspirations to be a developed economy by 2020 depend to a large extent on the development of technological capabilities that are in turn dependent on learning from the multinationals operating in the country. Therefore, increasing inflows of FDI remain to this day an important goal in the country.

The need for FDI also prompted Malaysia to agree to the merger of the AIA Agreement with the ASEAN Investment Guarantee Agreement into a single comprehensive investment agreement or the ASEAN Comprehensive Investment Agreement (ACIA) in 2009. The global financial crisis in 2009 heightened the competitive global environment for FDI, and the ACIA was crafted with the aim to create a more liberalized investment regime based on international best practices (Chaisse and Hamanaka 2014). Toward this end, the ACIA grants immediate benefits to ASEAN investors and ASEAN-based foreign investors, thereby removing the priority given to ASEAN investors in the AIA for the period 2003–2010. It also has an expanded scope as it covers both FDI and portfolio investment as compared to FDI only in the AIA. The ACIA, in addition, has more comprehensive and clear provisions for investment protection, a more comprehensive dispute settlement mechanism, and an earlier deadline to achieve free and open investment by 2015 compared to the AIA. Its impact on investment, however, remains to be seen, since it only took effect in March 2012.

In the case of services liberalization, eight packages of services liberalization have been signed to date, covering 96 subsectors with the aim of increasing the coverage to another 32 subsectors by 2015, making a total of 128 subsectors (Arizal 2014). There are ongoing efforts to liberalize autonomously, with the first package announced in 2009 allowing for 100% foreign equity ownership in 27 services subsectors and a second package announced in 2011. However, the focus of these liberalization efforts on increasing sector coverage and foreign equity ownership is insufficient as the services sector is governed by regulatory measures for protecting the consumer due to information asymmetries. At the same time, these same measures may serve as entry barriers to both domestic and foreign service providers, be it intentionally or unintentionally. The overall Services Trade Restrictiveness Index score of Malaysia is 46.1, which is higher than the overall ASEAN average score of 43.8, excluding Singapore (Sauve 2013). This indicates that deepening liberalization in services will require Malaysia to address the regulatory measures that are restricting entry. The lack of transparency in the implementation of preferential policies in the services sector and the preferential policies of GLCs that prevail in this sector makes it difficult to ascertain the extent to which these policies have affected the liberalization of the sector.

The AEC also addressed concerns about the widening development gap between the older member states and the CLMV countries (Cambodia, the Lao People's Democratic Republic, Myanmar, and Viet Nam). Strategies for narrowing the development divide include the Initiative for ASEAN Integration (IAI) that was launched in 2000 as a framework for regional cooperation whereby the more developed ASEAN members could help those member states that most need it (Severino 2007). Malaysia supported this initiative based on Mahathir's Prosper-Thy-Neighbour policy, where he noted that "prosperous neighbours make good trading partners and give each other less problems... We should actively help each other. Certainly the newer members of our Association are going need help in order to catch up with the older members" (Mahathir in keynote address, ASEAN Secretariat, undated).

Since the IAI projects entailed mostly studies and training, they fitted well into the Malaysian Technical Cooperation Programme, launched in 1980 to support technical cooperation with other developing countries. In fact, by the time the IAI was launched, Malaysia had acquired over 2 decades of experience in capacity development for developing countries and could draw on this experience to support the IAI programs (Tham and Kwek 2007). In the Ninth Malaysia Plan, it was noted that Malaysia spent a total of RM5.8 million to narrow the development divide. Funston (1998) further observed that Malaysia as well as Singapore and Thailand, contributed millions of dollars annually for other forms of direct assistance to the CLMV countries to help their governments.

ASEAN-Plus

Malaysia's main trading partners were Japan, the US, and Singapore, until the PRC took over as the leading trading partner from 2010 onward. ASEAN's external trade relations with the world hold particular importance for Malaysia because of its dependence on external trade due to the limited size of its domestic market.

Malaysia's focus on East Asia can be traced back to Mahathir's proposal for an East Asian regional grouping in 1990. This was driven by the lack of progress in the General Agreement on Tariffs and Trade Uruguay Round ministerial meeting in December 1990. Mahathir thus proposed the formation of a regional trade grouping, comprising ASEAN member states; the PRC; Hong Kong, China; Japan; and the Republic of Korea—or the East Asia Economic Group—in 1990. Mahathir's objective was to establish a regional trade arrangement for the group in response to the emergence of preferential regional trade arrangements elsewhere, including in North America, and to exercise a global impact on trade issues modeled after the Cairns Group (Kawai 2007). However, such a grouping would have excluded major and powerful trading partners such as the US. The proposal was deemed to be retaliatory in nature; motivated by a fear that economic regionalism would be dominated by the West (Buszynski 1998; Terada 2003). It certainly did not appear to consider the importance of the US as Malaysia's second largest trading partner in 1990, after Japan, and its potential repercussions on US–Malaysia trade. Given the importance of US trade with other ASEAN member states and objections from the US, it was not surprising that there was no consensus within ASEAN on the proposal. As a concession to Mahathir, ASEAN did eventually accept the idea of the East Asia Economic Group, but it was renamed the East Asia Economic Caucus as it was to be a caucus within the Asia-Pacific Economic Cooperation (APEC) forum. The key players outside ASEAN such as Japan were also hesitant in its support due to US opposition and its strategic priority on the emerging APEC process, while the PRC reportedly took a cautious approach (Kawai 2007). Interest in the East Asia Economic Caucus proposal eventually waned in the absence of support from key countries in Northeast Asia.

Nevertheless, the idea of an East Asian regional grouping did gradually take root through a series of informal discussions, and an invitation was issued by Singapore Prime Minister Goh Chok Tong to the three Northeast Asian countries to ASEAN's informal summit meeting within 1 or 1.5 years' time from 1995. Essentially a de facto ASEAN Plus Three process started when the leaders of the PRC, Japan, and the Republic of Korea were invited to the informal ASEAN leaders' meeting in December 1997, in the midst of the Asian financial crisis (Kawai 2007). The ASEAN Plus Three was subsequently formally launched in April 1999 (Terada 2003). Thus, the East Asia Economic Caucus proposal may be seen as a precursor to the ASEAN Plus Three process, as membership of the latter overlaps with that of the former.

Almost a decade later, Mahathir's successor, Abdullah Badawi, resurrected the idea of an East Asian Community at the 2004 ASEAN Plus Three (PRC, Japan, and Republic of Korea) meeting, and immediately won the backing from the PRC's Premier Wen Jiabao. The First East Asia Summit was convened in December 2005 and the Kuala Lumpur Declaration on the East Asia Summit indicated that it will be "a forum for dialogue on broad strategic, political and economic issues of common interest and concern with the aim of promoting peace, stability and economic prosperity in East Asia" (ASEAN Secretariat 2005). Therefore, although a regional trade arrangement was not formed, a regional grouping comprising by and large the countries suggested by Mahathir did materialize.

7.3   Future Directions

Malaysia was the chair of ASEAN in 2015. Former Prime Minister Najib chose "People-centered ASEAN" as the theme for that year as he envisaged a more direct involvement of all sectors of society rather than ASEAN being for the elites and specialists alone (*New Straits Times* 2014). This emphasis on the peoples of ASEAN and their well-being was subsequently included in the ASEAN 2025 Vision that was endorsed by the leaders at their 27th Summit for charting the direction forward for ASEAN up to 2025.

Domestically, as mentioned earlier, growth faltered after a decade of high uninterrupted growth before the emergence of the AFC (Table 7.1). In the 10 years or so after the AFC, Malaysia's growth dipped twice: 2001 and 2009 recorded negative growth. Concern over the reduced growth momentum led to a slew of government initiatives in 2010 to reinvigorate the economy. The government launched the New Economic Model (NEM) for Malaysia in its drive to propel the country toward a high-income economy. The ultimate goal of the NEM is to improve the quality of life of Malaysians by targeting a high per capita income of $15,000–$20,000 by 2020 that is also inclusive and sustainable (NEAC 2010). The new economy is envisaged to be one that is "… market-led, well-governed, regionally integrated, entrepreneurial and innovative" (NEAC 2010: 14). Eight strategic reform initiatives are identified in the NEM as the foundational measures for restructuring the economy. These are (i) re-energizing the private sector; (ii) developing a quality workforce; (iii) developing a competitive domestic economy; (iv) strengthening the public sector; (v) transparent and market-friendly affirmative action; (vi) building knowledge base infrastructure; (vii) enhancing sources of growth; and (viii) ensuring sustainability of growth. Although the NEM does not reject affirmative action, it has emphasized the need for these actions to be transparent and market-friendly, with a specific focus on the bottom 40% of households.

To facilitate the transformation of the economy, a government transformation program was introduced to strengthen public services and to facilitate the shift of the government as an enabler rather than as a driving force of growth. The plan focuses on six national key result areas: reducing crime, fighting corruption, improving student outcomes, raising living standards of low-income households, improving rural basic infrastructure, and improving urban public transport.

The Economic Transformation Programme (ETP) was launched in September 2010 as the road map for increasing private investment in the country (Government of Malaysia 2010). The ETP targets 12 growth engines, called national key economic areas, that are chosen in consultation with the private sector, to drive economic activity from 2010 to 2020. The 12 areas are oil, gas, and energy; palm oil; financial services; tourism; business services; electronics and electrical; wholesale and retail; education; health care; communications content and infrastructure; agriculture; and Greater Kuala Lumpur and Klang Valley. Potential investments in these 12 key economic areas are identified as 131 entry point projects, which are the focal points of the ETP. The ETP plan acknowledges the need for enabling actions such as promoting private investment, growing human capital, improving the business environment, and investing in infrastructure. The ETP is also premised on private investment, as the private sector is expected to contribute as much as 92% of the total projected investment of RM1.4 trillion needed to shift Malaysia to a high-income economy (Government of Malaysia 2010). Public funding is expected to be only 8% while investment from the private sector is expected to increase from

RM72 billion in 2010 to RM120 billion per year. Domestic investment is expected to contribute 73% of the total private investment, while the remaining 27% is expected to be contributed by FDI. It should be noted that Malaysia considers investment from the GLCs as private investment. As of 2011, PEMANDU (or the Performance, Management and Delivery Unit that is tasked to implement and monitor the ETP) has reported RM114 million of investment from the government and GLCs and RM62 million from the private sector, indicating that public investment (including the GLCs) is still dominating investment in the country (Ong and Teh 2012). FDI has reportedly recovered, increasing by 12.3% from RM29.3 billion in 2010 to RM32.9 billion in 2011, dropping slightly to RM32.12 billion in 2012 in line with the global drop in manufacturing.

The Tenth Malaysia Plan (2011-2015) launched in 2010 and the Eleventh Malaysia Plan (2016-2020) launched in 2015 essentially embrace the eight strategic reform initiatives as structural reforms needed under the two respective plan periods. They are both premised and focused on the six national key result areas of the government transformation program and the 12 national key economic areas of the ETP.

All these initiatives indicate a government that is cognizant of the current growth challenges that are related to the underlying restructuring problems in the country. The ASEAN market continues to hold an important position in Malaysia's economic transformation as it will enable the country's domestic firms to overcome a relatively small domestic market and gain economies of scale by venturing into the regional market. ASEAN's flexible approach towards economic cooperation and integration is also in line with Malaysia's policy stance. As noted by Sta. Maria, who was the secretary general of the Ministry of International Trade and Industry in 2015, rules and regulations are the biggest challenges in the development of the AEC. Malaysia has always prioritized what it deems to be fair trade, which can provide the space for the growth of sectors that are considered to be strategic and important for the country's growth due to their beneficial economic spinoffs besides ensuring a balance in the socioeconomic development of the country (EUMCCI 2014). This meets the requirements of balancing the trade needs with the domestic affirmative actions of the country.

The reduced growth momentum of the country while setting high goals such as achieving high income by 2020, in the midst of restructuring problems (Hal et al. 2012), has led Malaysia to embark on even more bilateral FTAs, besides pressing forward with the forging of an ASEAN Economic

Community.[3] This includes the decision to participate in the negotiations for the Trans-Pacific Partnership (TPP) Agreement in 2010 despite the failure to conclude an FTA with the US in 2007 and the well-known comprehensive nature of the agreement. The TPP Agreement includes, among others, the thorny government procurement issue that was one of the contributory factors to the breakdown of the Malaysia–US Free Trade Agreement. The Ministry of International Trade and Industry, however, in its brief on the TPP, asserts that the three objectives of the TPP— trade and investment liberalization, the development of transparent and predictable rules and disciplines, as well as a more transparent and inclusive regulatory environment—are in line with the economic transformation and domestic reform programs of Malaysia (MITI undated). The Ministry of International Trade and Industry also posited four strategic rationales for joining the TPP: market access; attracting investment, including investment from non-TPP countries wanting to base their operations in Malaysia to enjoy the benefits of TPP; engaging with TPP countries that currently do not have a bilateral FTA with Malaysia, such as the US, Canada, Mexico, and Peru; and lowering the cost of production by taking advantage of competition and economies of scale offered in the TPP. Malaysia thus signed the agreement in February 2016 with the other 11 founding members. However, the agreement has not yet been ratified as of 2018.

The 14th General Elections (GE14) in May 2018 led to an unprecedented change as the then opposition party won, leading to a change in government for the first time since independence. But the return of Mahathir as the seventh Prime Minister has reversed the previous policy of cautious liberalization with a shift towards greater nationalistic sentiments. Mahathir has called for a review of the new TPP agreement, or the Comprehensive and Progressive Agreement for Trans-Pacific Partnership (CPTPP), with the withdrawal of the US from the original agreement (The Star Online 12 June 2018). Malaysia is also a party to the ongoing negotiations for a Regional Comprehensive Economic Partnership Agreement (RCEP), which may be looked upon more favorably by the current regime since it is more in line with Mahathir's preference for a "Look East" position because it engages Japan, the Republic of Korea, and the People's Republic of China. It is also unlikely that the RCEP will be achieve deep liberalization, given ASEAN's own pace of liberalization.

---

[3]   External pressures have also contributed to the shift to bilateral and regional liberalization, including among others, the stalled multilateral liberalization in the Doha Round and the bandwagon effect from Singapore's shift to bilateral FTAs.

7.4   Conclusion

Although Malaysia's interest in ASEAN was originally motivated by geopolitical considerations, it progressively began to see the potential of an enlarged ASEAN market for the country's economic gains. As the economy grew and prospered, Malaysia has also been willing to share resources for capacity building with the newer ASEAN member states for furthering economic integration. Domestically, however, economic redistributive policies impinge on Malaysia's participation in ASEAN's integration process. At the same time, growth targets that are needed to meet the high-income agenda of the government dictates further liberalization and integration with regional value chains. ASEAN has the potential to position itself strategically if there is cohesive economic integration with an enlarged, seamlessly integrated ASEAN market. Thus, Malaysia's trade policy has to straddle two conflicting objectives—one that demands at least progressive liberalization, while domestic politics point to protectionist tendencies at odds with an increasingly globally integrated world governed by network trade. Moreover, progressive liberalization is no longer about mere market access alone. The reach of trade liberalization now extends far beyond border issues to behind-the-border barriers, especially on rules and regulations that restrict trade and confer advantages to privileged groups.

ASEAN's flexible approach toward liberalization and even more flexible implementation of its commitments suited Malaysia's preferred pace of liberalization under the previous Najib regime. Malaysia's rethinking of its liberalization commitments and its veering toward anti-globalization sentiments under the new government elected in 2018 implies that Malaysia is unlikely to press for a more rules-based ASEAN. Malaysia will continue to support flexibility in liberalization commitments as well as in the implementation of ASEAN's commitments.

References

Arizal, T.S. 2014. Liberalization of Services Sector in Malaysia. www.smecorp.gov.my/vn2/sites/default/files/Presentations_MITI.pdf.

ASEAN Secretariat. 2005. Kuala Lumpur Declaration on the East Asia Summit Kuala Lumpur, 14 December 2005. Jakarta. http://www.asean.org/news/item/kuala-lumpur-declaration-on-the-east-asia-summit-kuala-lumpur-14-december-2005.

ASEAN Secretariat. 1997. ASEAN Economic Cooperation: Transition and Transformation. Jakarta.

ASEAN Secretariat. undated. History. The Founding of ASEAN. http://asean.org/asean/about-asean/history/.

ASEAN Secretariat. undated. Keynote Address by The Honourable Dato' Seri Dr. Mahathir Mohamed The Prime Minister of Malaysia. http://www.asean.org/communities/asean-political-security-community/item/keynote-address-by-the-honourable-dato-seri-dr-mahathir-mohamed-the-prime-minister-of-malaysia.

Athukorala, P.C. 2012. Malaysian Economy in Three Crises. In H. Hill, S.Y. Tham, and H.M.Z. Ragayah, eds. *Malaysia's Development Challenges: Graduating from the Middle*. Abingdon: Routledge Malaysian Studies Series.

Bende-Nabebde, A. 2001. FDI, Regional Economic Integration and Endogenous Growth, Some evidence from Southeast Asia. *Pacific Economic Review* 6(3): 383–399.

Buzynski, L. 1998. ASEAN's New Challenges. *Pacific Affairs* 70(4): 555–577.

Chaisse, J., and S. Hamanaka. 2014. The Investment Version of the Asian Noodle Bowl: The Proliferation of International Investment Agreements. *ADB Working Paper Series on Regional Economic Integration* No. 128. Manila: ADB.

Department of Statistics, Malaysia. Time Series Data. https://www.dosm.gov.my/v1/index.php?r=column/ctimeseries&menu_id=NHJlaGc2RI g4ZXlGTjh1SU1kaWY5UT09 (accessed 16 August 2018).

Department of Statistics, Malaysia. The Performance of the State's Economy, 2017. https://www.dosm.gov.my/v1/index.php?r=column/cthemeByCat&cat=449&bul_id=L25EUXQxbWdBaEVoWXU5aTF QWUpNdz09&menu_id=TE5CRUZCblh4ZTZMODZIbmk2aWRR QT09 (accessed 16 August 2018).

EU--Malaysia Chamber of Commerce & Industry (EUMCCI). Review. 2014. Cover Story: ASEAN Economic Community 2015: What It Means for Malaysia. *EUMCCI Review* Vol. 2 (2): 4–7.

Fitfield, R.H. 1979. National and Regional Interests in ASEAN: Competition and Cooperation in International Politics. *ISEAS Occasional Paper* No. 57. Singapore: Institute of Southeast Asian Studies.

Funston, J. 1998. ASEAN: Out of Its Depth? *Contemporary Southeast Asia* 20(1): 22–37.

Government of Malaysia. 2010. Economic Transformation Programme (ETP). etp.pemandu.gov.my/Download_Centre-@-Download_Centre.aspx.

Hal, H., S.Y. Tham, and H.M.Z. Ragayah (eds.) 2012. *Malaysia's Development Challenges: Graduating from the Middle.* Abingdon: Routledge Malaysian Studies Series.

Jarvis, D.S. 2012. Foreign Direct Investment & Investment Liberalization in Asia: Assessing ASEAN's Initiatives. *Australian Journal of International Affairs* 66(2): 223–264.

Intal, P. Jr. et al. 2014. *ASEAN Rising: ASEAN and AEC Beyond 2015.* Jakarta: Economic Research Institute for ASEAN and East Asia.

Kawai, M. 2007. Evolving Economic Architecture in East Asia. *ADBI Discussion Paper* No. 84. Tokyo: Asian Development Bank Institute.

Kurus, B. 1993. Agreeing to Disagree: The Political Reality of ASEAN Economic Cooperation. *Asian Affairs: An American Review* 20(1): 28–44.

Marwah, K., and A. Tavakoli. 2004. The Effects of Foreign Capital and Imports on Economic Growth. *Journal of Asian Economics* 15: 399–413.

Masron, T.A., and Z. Yusop. 2012. The ASEAN Investment Area, Other FDI Initiatives, and Intra–ASEAN Foreign Direct Investment. *Asian-Pacific Economic Literature* 26(2): 88–103. http://dx.doi.org/10.1111/j.1467-8411.2012.01346.x.

Ministry of International Trade and Industry (MITI). Undated. Brief on the Trans-Pacific Partnership (TPP).

Menon, J. 2014. Malaysia's Investment Malaise: What Happened and Can It Be Fixed. In S.B. Das and P.O. Lee, eds. *Malaysia's Socio-Economic*

Transformation: Ideas for the Next Decade. Singapore: Institute of Southeast Asian Studies.

National Economic Advisory Council (NEAC). 2010. *New Economic Model for Malaysia" Part 1: Strategic Policy Directions*. Putrajaya.

Nesadurai, H.E.S. 2003. *Globalisation, Domestic Politics and Regionalism: The ASEAN Free Trade Area*. London: Routledge.

Ong, K.M., and C.C. Teh. 2012. A Critique of the ETP: Part 4 – Enterprise – Private Enterprises Are Rejecting the ETP. *Focus Paper 2012/02/15*. Kuala Lumpur: Research for Social Advancement.

New Straits Times. 2014. Create People-Centered ASEAN. 9 April. http://www2.nst.com.my/nation/general/create-people-centred-asean-1.557159/facebook-comments-7.813226 (accessed 29 November 2014).

Postigo, A. 2013. Negotiating Protection under Overlapping Free Trade Agreements: Dynamic Interplay between Free Trade Agreements and Investment. *Working Paper Series* No. 13-150. London: Development Studies Institute, London School of Economics and Political Science.

Ravenhill, J. 1995. Economic Cooperation in Southeast Asia: Changing Incentives. *Asian Survey* 35(9): 850–866.

Sauve, P. 2013. Services Trade and the ASEAN Community. http://aienetwork.org/speaker-series/005-pierre-sauve/services-trade-and-the-asean-economic-community-pierre-sauve.pdf (accessed 29 November 2014).

Severino, R. 2007. The ASEAN Development Divide and the Initiative for ASEAN Integration. *ASEAN Economic Bulletin* 24(1): 35–44.

The Star Online 2014. SPAD: All New Taxis to Be Brown Proton Exora Starting Nov. 1. 30 April. http://www.thestar.com.my/News/Nation/2014/04/30/All-Taxis-Exora/ (accessed 29 November 2014).

The Star Online 2018. *No need to be alarmed just yet*. https://www.thestar.com.my/news/nation/2018/06/12/no-need-to-be-alarmed-just-yet-the-prime-ministers-call-for-a-review-will-give-a-chance-for-malaysia/ (accessed 16 August 2018).

Terada, T. 2003. Constructing an "East Asian" Concept and Growing Regional Identity: from EAEC to ASEAN+3. *The Pacific Review* 16(2): 251–277.

Tham, S.Y. 2004. Malaysian Policies for the Automobile Sector: Focus in Technology Transfer. In R. Busser and Y. Sadoi, eds. *Production Networks in Asia and Europe: Skill Formation and Technology Transfer in the Automobile Industry*. London: Routledge Curzon.

Tham, S.Y., and K.T. Kwek. 2007. Prosper-Thy-Neighbour Policies: Malaysia's Contributions after the Asian Financial Crisis. *ASEAN Economic Bulletin* 24(1): 72–97.

Yoshimutsu, H. 2002. Preferences, Interests and Regional Integration: The Development of the ASEAN Industrial Cooperation Arrangement. *Review of International Political Economy* 9(1): 123–149.

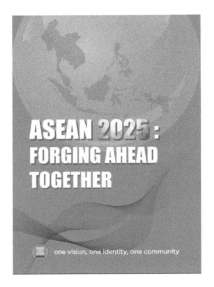
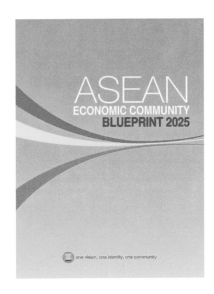

Charting a course for ASEAN Integration. ASEAN's efforts at achieving integration have been guided by blueprints that set the targets and timetables for implementation (covers of ASEAN 2025 and blueprints from the ASEAN Secretariat website, https://asean.org/).

CHAPTER 8

GEARING THE PHILIPPINES FOR THE ASEAN ECONOMIC COMMUNITY

Florian A. Alburo

This chapter highlights differences in the establishment of the European Community and ASEAN. It also explores the Philippines' readiness for the ASEAN Economic Community.

Introduction

This chapter argues that the way for the Philippines to the ASEAN Economic Community (AEC) is not through the Association of Southeast Asian Nations (ASEAN) but through the world. Being good neighbors will define the AEC and how the Philippines fits into it—not necessarily in the way it was planned. The Philippines has always been an ardent subscriber to ASEAN throughout its evolution. In the economic sphere, the Philippines has always adhered to all economic cooperation modalities (at times even aggressively), participated in various ASEAN projects, and contributed to regional gatherings that examine and plot ASEAN's course. Yet, the Philippines' ASEAN-ness has hardly been evident in its trade with other ASEAN members.[1]

Circumstances have changed dramatically since ASEAN was founded; many of these circumstances have shaped the region and influenced how it may eventually evolve as a community. At the ASEAN Summit in December 1997, ASEAN adopted Vision 2020 which sees "...a stable, prosperous, and highly competitive ASEAN economic region in which there is a free flow of goods, services, investment, and freer flow of capital, equitable economic development and reduced poverty and socio-economic disparities..." by 2020. Subsequently, the ASEAN leaders signed the Declaration of ASEAN Concord II (Bali Concord II) in October 2003 for the AEC as the goal of economic integration. The ASEAN Summit in December 2005 considered accelerating the AEC from 2020 to 2015 and requested concerned

---

[1] Over many decades, ASEAN's share of Philippine trade hardly reached more than 15% (although the same can be said of ASEAN as a whole).

ministers to examine the possibility. The ASEAN Secretariat was asked to develop a single and coherent blueprint for advancing the AEC from 2020 to 2015, with clear targets and time lines. The ministers recommended the acceleration of the AEC and proposed it to the ASEAN Summit in January 2007. This 12th ASEAN Summit approved the acceleration of the AEC and the 13th ASEAN Summit adopted the AEC Blueprint. If we trace the evolution of this "marching order" for ASEAN (which also defines how the Philippines fits), a distinct break is evident.

A number of studies list the different ASEAN economic agreements that are supposed to contribute to trade among the member states and further integration of their economies (Chia 2004; Cuyvers, De Lombaerde, and Verherstraeten 2005; Nandan 2006). These studies often classify the agreements according to the members that participate, their status, or according to the kind of agreement (e.g., goods, services, investment). A more comprehensive list can be found at the ASEAN Secretariat, which lists more than 325 ASEAN treaties and agreements since its founding in 1967. About 50 of these are in the form of economic agreements that seek to promote greater trade within ASEAN.[2] While there are others that could also be considered economic agreements, these do not really address a change in the economic environment in which traders, producers, and consumers alter their behavior—for example, agreements to establish an ASEAN center, undertake cooperation (agriculture cooperatives, environment, energy), ASEAN declarations, and some memoranda. In fact, such a list includes many that do not require ratification by the member states.[3]

What may be useful is to understand the character of these agreements as they have evolved over time. The original rationale for the establishment of ASEAN was as a security alliance. Moving into the economic field, and a more regional development direction, was obviously not usual fare to the members. In fact, the language of the Treaty of Amity and Cooperation in Southeast Asia remained couched in terms of regional peace and stability, even if the economic provisions alluded to promoting economic growth in the region, expansion of trade, and improvement of economic infrastructure (e.g., Article 6 of the Treaty, 1976). The Bali Concord of 1976, though clearly indicating the importance of industrial and trade cooperation, remained

---

[2]   This number is purely arbitrary and based on a simple cursory review of all the treaties and agreements which have been catalogued in ASEAN.

[3]   Strictly speaking, if we go by definition of an agreement as requiring ratification, then such a listing would be more accurate.

focused on stability and the elimination of threats posed by subversion to its stability. Note, however, that even then the Bali Concord was already urging member states to develop an awareness of regional identity and create a strong ASEAN community (1976 Declaration of ASEAN Concord, No. 8).

First of all, the evolution of ASEAN economic agreements may be characterized as country-centered. The identification of regional industrial projects, the ASEAN Industrial Complementation, ASEAN Industrial Joint Ventures, ASEAN Preferential Trading Arrangement, and even the initial listing for the ASEAN Common Effective Preferential Tariff (CEPT) scheme all began at the country level. This is not to suggest that they should not have begun at the country level. However, many of these agreements did not really have regional reference points. As late as the CEPT scheme, each country simply determined what products it identified in its inclusion list; in earlier agreements, the countries identified their own regional industrial projects or industrial complementation. This was understandable since without a notion of regional markets or regional integration, the second-best option was a country-level determination (done mostly by bureaucrats).

Second, and related to the first, the content of the agreements was selective or fragmented. Especially in the early part of the evolution, the choices of products or sectors for liberalization or promotion were somewhat arbitrary. Those that fell under the inclusion list, exclusion list, or exception list were selective. In short, the selective nature of the content of the agreements appears to have been based on criteria that did not directly impact regional or intra-ASEAN economic transactions. This character is prominent in the early agreements relating to areas of economic cooperation during the 1980s.

Third, many of the recent economic agreements reflect deliberate responses to the changing global environment of ASEAN. In particular, the lack of success in getting the Doha Round completed has driven the region to seek more regional and intra-regional trade and other economic cooperation arrangements. This is reflected in the quickening pace of specific agreements. For instance, the ASEAN Framework Agreement on Services (AFAS) agreed on three rounds (between the fifth and the seventh rounds) in 3 years, whereas it took 7 years between the first and the third rounds. Similarly, many free trade agreements were initiated in a shorter span of time. In contrast, ASEAN took its time in responding to global changes in the early part of the evolution of its economic agreements.

For example, it took 15 years before the original ASEAN Preferential Trading Arrangement (APTA) was abandoned for the ASEAN Free Trade Area (AFTA) at a time when globalization was starting to pick up, multinational firms were breaking up production into different locations, and foreign investors were seeking active hosts for foreign capital. Indeed, many of the ASEAN member states may have missed significant opportunities for global economic participation by hinging their international participation on ASEAN. While the delay in response can be explained (e.g., lingering import substitution policies of some members), its muted impact on the region in terms of expanded intra-ASEAN trade was evident.

Finally, the increasing complexity, substantive content, and technical nature of the agreements have significantly benefited from improvements in the institutional capacity of the ASEAN Secretariat, which was reorganized under a 1992 amendment to the agreement establishing it. The formal recognition of the stature of the secretary-general (as a minister on par with the other ministers of ASEAN), the professionalization of the staff, and increased knowledge within the organization have all been instrumental in improving the caliber of the agreements. This is evident in a cursory reading of the agreements as they have evolved over time. Indeed, the AEC Blueprint is a product of the ASEAN Secretariat.

Table 8.1 lists the various general and specific agreements entered into by ASEAN that relate to the economy. Table 8.2 groups the various economic agreements in ASEAN in time periods. While Table 8.1 reveals that most of the economic areas are covered by the agreements (trade in goods, services, investment, etc.), Table 8.2 reveals that the evolution of the agreements has been somewhat arbitrary in terms of their time line. Notice the increasing sophistication of the agreements beginning in 2001, with more focus on the regional aspects or implications on intra-ASEAN trade. The agreements in the 1980s were more bureaucracy-driven, confined mostly to the development of the APTA as the initial means of economic cooperation and the pursuit of regional development. Table 8.3 focuses on the components of the economic agreements in terms of the AEC and their dates.

Table 8.1: Key ASEAN Agreements on Economic Integration

General

The ASEAN Declaration (Bangkok Declaration) Bangkok, 8 August 1967

Declaration of ASEAN Concord, Bali, 24 February 1976

Protocol to Amend the Framework Agreement on Enhancing ASEAN Economic Cooperation, Thailand, 15 December 1995

ASEAN Vision 2020, Kuala Lumpur, 15 December 1997

Hanoi Plan of Action, Hanoi, 15 December 1998

Hanoi Declaration on Narrowing the Development Gap for Closer ASEAN Integration, Hanoi, Viet Nam, 23 July 2001

Declaration of ASEAN Concord II (Bali Concord II), Bali, 7 October 2003

Vientiane Action Program 2004-10, Vientiane, 29 November 2004

Goods

Agreement on the ASEAN Preferential Trading Arrangement (1977)

Customs Code of Conduct (1983)

Agreement on the Common Effective Preferential Tariff Scheme for the ASEAN Free Trade Area (1992)

Customs Code of Conduct (1995)

ASEAN Agreement on Customs (1997)

ASEAN Customs Vision 2020 (1997)

ASEAN Framework Agreement on the Facilitation of Goods in Transit (1998)

ASEAN Framework Agreement on Mutual Recognition Arrangements (1998)

Guidelines for Mutual Assistance to Combat Customs Fraud and Smuggling (1998)

Protocol on the Special Arrangement for Sensitive and Highly Sensitive Products (1999)

ASEAN Customs Policy Implementation and Work Programme (1999)

Understanding on the Criteria for Classification in the ASEAN Harmonised Tariff Nomenclature (2003)

Services

ASEAN Framework Agreement on Services (1995)

Protocol to Amend the ASEAN Framework Agreement on Services (2003)

Investment

Framework Agreement on the ASEAN Investment Area (1998)

Protocol to Amend the Framework Agreement on the ASEAN Investment Area (2001)

continued on next page

Table 8.1 *continued*

Dispute Settlement
Protocol on Dispute Settlement Mechanism (1996)
ASEAN Protocol on Enhanced Dispute Settlement Mechanism (2004)

ASEAN = Association of Southeast Asian Nations.

Source: Nandan, G. 2006. *ASEAN: Building an Economic Community*. Canberra ACT, Australia: Department of Foreign Affairs and Trade, Economic Analytical Unit.

Table 8.2: Agreements and Time Lines

1980–1991
ASEAN Industrial Projects, ASEAN Industrial Complementation, ASEAN Industrial Joint Venture
Brand to Brand, Preferential Trade Arrangement (PTA)
Enhanced PTA
Customs Code of Conduct

1992–2000
Common Effective Preferential Tariff, ASEAN Framework Agreement on Services (AFAS), Mutual Recognition Arrangements, ASEAN Investment Area (AIA)
Agreement on Customs
Facilitation of Goods – Transit

2001–2004
AIA, ASEAN Free Trade Agreements (People's Republic of China, India, Japan, etc.)
ASEAN Concord II
Sectoral Integration

2005–2009
AFAS (5th, 6th, 7th)
ASEAN Single Window, ASEAN Plus Three
Free Trade Agreement, ASEAN Comprehensive Investment Agreement, ASEAN Trade in Goods Agreement

ASEAN = Association of Southeast Asian Nations.

Source: Author's classification.

Table 8.3: Illustrative Economic Agreements That Contribute
to Key Areas in the ASEAN Economic Community

1	Single Market and Production Base
	Flow of Goods – ASEAN Free Trade Area/Common Effective Preferential Tariff (1992, 2003), ASEAN Trade in Goods Agreement (2009), ASEAN Single Window (2005), Priority Integration Sectors (2008), Agreement on Customs, Free Trade Agreements (India, Republic of Korea, People's Republic of China, Australia/New Zealand)
	Flow of Services – ASEAN Framework Agreement on Services (AFAS) (1995, 2009), Mutual Recognition Arrangements (1996, 2007, 2008), Multilateral Agreement on the Full Liberalization of Air Freight Services (2009), Protocol on Unlimited Freedom Traffic Rights (2009), Financial Services Package in AFAS (2008)
	Flow of Investments – ASEAN Investment Area (1998), ASEAN Comprehensive Investment Agreement (2009)
	Flow of Capital
	Flow of Skilled Labor – Mutual Recognition Arrangements (1998, 2009)
2	Competitive Economic Region – Memorandum of Understanding
3	Equitable Economic Development – Initiative for ASEAN Integration
4	Integration into the Global Economy

ASEAN = Association of Southeast Asian Nations.

Source: Author's classification based on various ASEAN Secretariat reports.

Clearly, the evolution of ASEAN economic cooperation has been from one centered on countries to a more regional perspective; from one of grouping regional parameters to a vision of an integrated region. As shown in Table 8.3, ASEAN is viewed as single market and production base in terms of the flow of goods, services, investments, and skilled labor, integrated with the global economy, and as a region with more equitable development and competitiveness. This vision of the ASEAN region as a production base recognizes that in the current global environment, the region captures a significant slice of the global value chain. Yet, much of the region's ability to encompass global value chains depends not only on a regional agreement but on many dynamic factors, including technology and networked firms. Indeed as early as 1995, when AFTA was just beginning, the relevance of networks was raised in the context of regional economic cooperation (Alburo 1995).

8.1   Referencing Economic Community

This is the broad backdrop against which we examine the Philippines' readiness for the AEC. This section is a slight digression into the notion of an economic community. Reference is made to the European Economic Community (EEC), its similarities to the ASEAN evolution, and major differences in current practice. Recent developments in the EEC show weaknesses that were apparently glossed over in its enthusiasm. We argue that the meaning of "community" in the AEC needs qualification, especially when carried to its extreme, and that it would make sense to sort out issues that particularly impinge on the AEC.

The European Union (EU) is often considered as setting the bar for an economic community. The EU started out as the EEC (1957), later on transforming into a union, a single Europe (1986, 1992) and then a currency union (1999, 2002). Several things were happening in the EEC: southern enlargement, eastern enlargement, liberalized movement of labor, harmonization of product, safety, food regulations, etc. The parallels with ASEAN are clearly evident.

Like ASEAN, the EEC's primary impetus was peace and security. In fact, it really began as a coal and steel community pooling major war protagonists' production to solidify the region. It was also a project to bring democracy and prosperity to a war-torn continent. Succeeding parts of the project fell into place, particularly the customs union, the free movement of goods, and eventually factors of production. The culmination was of course the single currency, adopted by most of the European nations. The key outcomes of this economic community were the large amount (more than 75%) of intra-European trade, seamless nature of regional infrastructure, and the seeming convergence of financial markets (especially bond spreads).

The EEC became synonymous with a homogeneous economy—a single market. In its early period, many production bases were within the EEC. The emergence of the European Parliament as an institution gave the region the appropriate oversight machinery and soon moved to provide development resources to newer members (in reference to equitable economic development, one of the pillars of the AEC).

In the run-up to the EU crisis in 2009, the community's vulnerability surfaced. Whatever the primary causes, the crisis revealed that there really was no economic homogeneity. For example, bond spreads varied considerably after early convergence. The loss of currency independence for the countries in crisis (e.g., Greece, Spain, Ireland, Italy) reduced the policy adjustment space necessary for recovery (Krugman 2011) and exposed the weaknesses of a monetary union. Indeed, independent views argue that the EU single currency did not conform to the theoretical framework set out by Mundell (1961), particularly the assumptions of labor mobility and fiscal integration.

There are several reasons why the AEC is likely to evolve in a manner different from the EU. First, it is unlikely that a single production base can be built around ASEAN in the same way the EEC did in its early days. Given dynamic changes in technology, firm behavior and transactions, and general unpredictability of production location and trade, ASEAN may not be able to easily capture global value chains around the region. The single market part of the pillar seems achievable in the AEC with the ASEAN Trade in Goods Agreement aiming for dismantling residual tariffs as well as nontariff barriers. However, the single market has to overcome border barriers, which are often non-transparent. More importantly, these may not be easily removed without a uniform regional mechanism or strong intercountry coordination and may create glitches in electronic communications across National Single Windows. Second, there are early limits to mobility even for highly skilled labor, as evident in the EU's inability to see labor adjusting to country recessions. The reason is simply that cultural and linguistic differences constrain such an adjustment (Schirru 2014). Third, a community that would be true to its very name and core would aim for a single currency. There is no doubt that the EU will ensure that the euro survives (short of some members withdrawing from the union), but only after some members have endured long and inequitable pain and suffering (high unemployment, internal devaluation).

If the AEC is to be true to its very name and core, should it go likewise for a single currency? Finally, the other pillars in the AEC (competitive economic region, equitable economic development, and integration with the global economy) are subsumed in the EEC in its supranational status, which conveys regional authority through the Council of Ministers or the European Council to carry out concerted competition policy, consumer protection, affirmative action for small and medium-sized enterprises (SMEs) as part of equitable economic development, particularly for new EU members, and collective approaches to forging free trade areas and more recently "mega areas." Contrasting this with how these analogous pillars are to be pursued in the AEC, they would be scattered across members and their different agencies and instrumentalities.

In short, we must avoid drawing parallels between the EEC and the AEC and its component pillars, more so since the community environment in the ASEAN and EEC contexts presumably differ and have dramatically changed since ASEAN was founded, implying a different bar to define and achieve. The meaning and content of the AEC, therefore, have to be pinned down, in which case the notion of economic community is removed of reference to the EEC.

8.2   Philippine Readiness for the ASEAN Economic Community

The analysis of the Philippines' readiness for the AEC focuses primarily on the first pillar—single market and production base trade in goods. We argue that while there are pockets of readiness, especially in an ex post sense, many of these hold true even without ASEAN. In fact, in drawing its CEPT schedules, the Philippines' tariff reduction path was lower than the ASEAN average. It had a limited exclusion list and adopted a program for reducing nontariff barriers. Many of the liberalization measures were of course global and not catered to ASEAN. Yet, like other ASEAN economic outcomes, the country's trade with ASEAN did not accelerate, Form D utilization rates were low, and in tracing releases of cargo, those from ASEAN were slower than those from other source countries (SATMP 2003).

Numerous awareness campaigns, studies, outreach programs, and assistance initiatives have been undertaken in the Philippines to enhance its readiness for the AEC. Analysis by Habito (2014) suggests that in the years prior to the launch of the AEC, the economy was starting to break out of its past patterns of spurts of growth and decline and the inability to create a momentum and sustain economic performance. However, it is unclear whether this was derived from or influenced transactions within ASEAN. The recent aggregate economic record does not suggest that it has been caused by ASEAN economic transactions or that it has influenced such transactions. For example, between 2015 and 2017, GDP growth was sustained and the country's total trade with ASEAN expanded despite a drag in overall trade growth. But growth was likewise sustained in 2012–2014, yet total ASEAN trade hardly moved even if overall trade expanded. These 3-year snippets and the longer term trend do not seem to evince a strong rooted behavior.

To examine this further, we trace the behavior of Philippine trade with ASEAN—historical magnitudes and growth—and compare this with extra-ASEAN trade. In terms of the AEC, we hypothesize the expected behavioral changes in the area of Philippine exports to ASEAN and its imports from the region. Figure 8.1a shows the Philippines' trade with ASEAN and its merchandise exports from 1992 to 2000. This is as reference for Figure 8.1b, which shows the magnitude of total Philippine merchandise exports and imports from 2000 to 2017 and the country's trade (merchandise exports and imports) with the nine other ASEAN member states for the same period. Notice that Philippine merchandise trade with ASEAN is a mirror image of its total trade with the world; this is especially evident during the financial crisis of 2009, when world trade collapsed. What is interesting is that there is a perceptible break from 2010, when there appears to be an acceleration of global imports relative to global exports (thus widening the trade deficit). Yet the country's ASEAN trade does not mirror this break in merchandise imports from other member states, which flattened during 2010–2012, thus reducing its regional trade deficit. The same can be said for 2003 when the trade deficit started to open up.

Philippine trade with ASEAN was fairly stable for nearly a decade (2000–2009), except for the noticeable break beginning 2010. Figure 8.1a traces an accelerating path of Philippine exports to ASEAN, when AFTA started, and even during the Asian financial crisis of 1997 (showing a fall in imports from ASEAN). Philippine exports to ASEAN followed a trajectory similar to overall exports, even slightly surpassing them toward the end of the decade.

Since the AEC envisions complete liberalization of all goods traded among the ASEAN member states, there are fears that a surge of intra-ASEAN imports will take place. These fears seem unfounded in the case of the Philippines. First, the pace and pattern of the country's trade with ASEAN member states shown in Figure 8.1 indicate that intra-ASEAN trade has been subdued relative to global trade. It is true that there has been a surge of imports from ASEAN since 2015 (until 2017) at 10% per year as shown in Figure 8.1 (b) but overall imports have also surged, though at a lower rate of 8.3% annually. Again, it is still premature to consider this as a significant effect of the AEC.

Second, historically, ASEAN's share of Philippine exports or imports has never exceeded 20% (between 1993 and 2012) and is the lowest among the ASEAN-6 (Brunei Darussalam, Indonesia, Malaysia, the Philippines, Singapore, and Thailand). Figure 8.2 shows the average shares to country totals of extra- and intra-ASEAN exports and imports in 2015. To expect

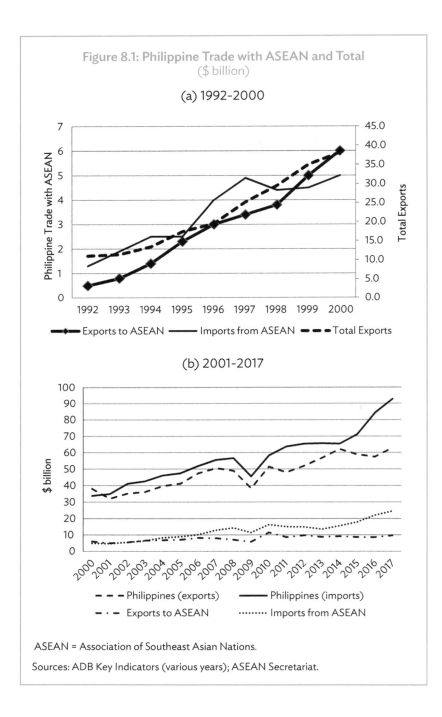

Figure 8.1: Philippine Trade with ASEAN and Total
($ billion)

(a) 1992-2000

Exports to ASEAN ━━━ **Imports from ASEAN** ━ ━ **Total Exports**

(b) 2001-2017

━ ━ Philippines (exports)   ━━━ Philippines (imports)
━ ･ ━ Exports to ASEAN   ········· Imports from ASEAN

ASEAN = Association of Southeast Asian Nations.

Sources: ADB Key Indicators (various years); ASEAN Secretariat.

this share to sharply rise for the Philippines because of the AEC is highly unlikely. It is also true that the country's most favored nation (MFN) rates have been falling almost in tandem with CEPT rates, reducing possible trade diversion. As Calvo-Pardo, Freund, and Ornelas (2009) have argued, AFTA has improved welfare in ASEAN in general and perhaps the Philippines in particular. This may also partly explain the stable share of the region's trade to total trade.

Third, there seems to be little room for more liberalization vis-à-vis ASEAN in terms of tariff rate reductions. On the one hand, between the original CEPT time line of 15 years (1993–2008) and the accelerated CEPT in 10 years (1993–2003), the Philippines (as well as the rest of the ASEAN-6) changed its tariffs to meet the original target of 0%–5% rates. On the other hand, the Philippines had a more aggressive reduction in the accelerated program. Consequently, the room for further reduction narrowed between the original and accelerated CEPT. These are averages, however, and there are clearly individual tariff lines for which further reduction is always possible, especially for interrelated lines. Indeed, disparities in some tariff lines in the accelerated CEPT across ASEAN member states indicate wide differences for some product lines, limiting market access for the Philippines or giving other ASEAN members wider access to the country. What is evident is that the commitment to liberalization in terms of average tariff rates still varies widely among specific lines. In short, it appears that the CEPT rates were not sufficiently rationalized. Figure 8.3 shows the CEPT rates for the ASEAN-6—original (Figure 8.3a) and the accelerated (Figure 8.3b).

Finally, it seems that the AEC instrument for trade in goods is quite complete with the CEPT rates reaching their targets. The path to zero tariffs in 2015 would be rather incremental and may not really have significantly distorted effects for the Philippines. By default, the Philippines' readiness for the AEC was set way back in 1993, throughout the period of the accelerated program.[4] Access to Philippine markets of products that were previously in the exclusion list may lead to spikes in their imports, which may threaten domestic substituting industries. The country's readiness for this was also set in 1993, when focus was given to items in the exclusion list, systematically assessing their competitiveness and considering alternatives, including adjustment mechanisms when their liberalization (in 2015) shall have taken place.

---

[4]   This is of course not totally true since the country still had exclusion lists (temporary, sensitive, and general), which would be completely gone in the AEC. This may be critical for some products such as unprocessed agricultural products.

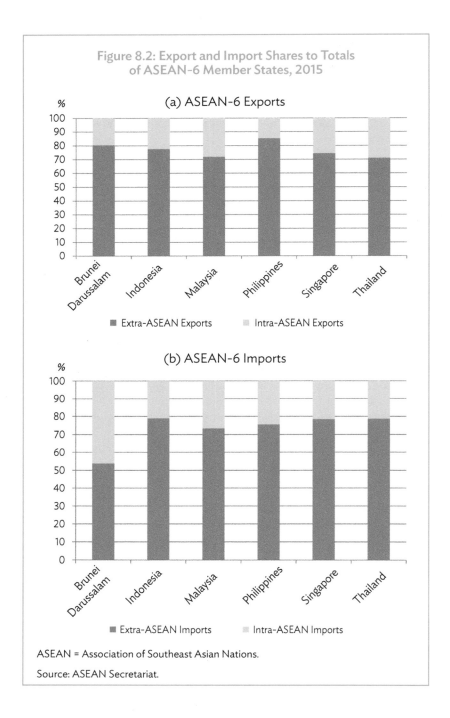

Figure 8.2: Export and Import Shares to Totals
of ASEAN-6 Member States, 2015

(a) ASEAN-6 Exports

■ Extra-ASEAN Exports   ■ Intra-ASEAN Exports

(b) ASEAN-6 Imports

■ Extra-ASEAN Imports   ■ Intra-ASEAN Imports

ASEAN = Association of Southeast Asian Nations.

Source: ASEAN Secretariat.

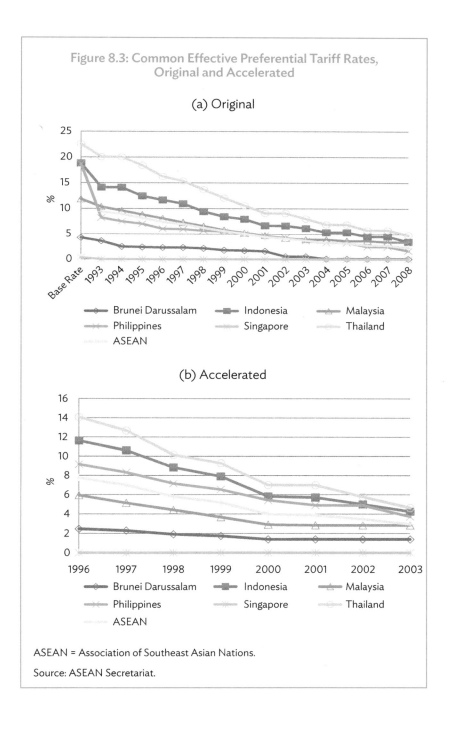

Figure 8.3: Common Effective Preferential Tariff Rates, Original and Accelerated

(a) Original

Legend: Brunei Darussalam, Indonesia, Malaysia, Philippines, Singapore, Thailand, ASEAN

(b) Accelerated

Legend: Brunei Darussalam, Indonesia, Malaysia, Philippines, Singapore, Thailand, ASEAN

ASEAN = Association of Southeast Asian Nations.

Source: ASEAN Secretariat.

As shown in Figure 8.1, while imports from ASEAN, on average, seem to have spiked in the last 3 years, overall imports also rose. Overall trade in the three years before the AEC is similar to the country's experience in the last 3 years of the 1990s. Depending on the magnitudes of trade in products in the exclusion list and the weight of ASEAN sources, what is more relevant to see is the readiness of the country to expand its exports to the region, which happened in the earlier period (see Figure 8.1a), not in the latter. This needs further investigation. With the extended experience of the country in AFTA, and in the run-up to the AEC, it is possible to hypothesize why Philippine–ASEAN trade has leveled off and where the country can pay attention to improve readiness. This would be particularly important given the apparent surge in the years 2015-2017.

Given the length of time of AFTA implementation, the apparent stable product menu traded with ASEAN member states, and the tandem decline in MFN tariff rates, ASEAN markets have probably matured in terms of product preferences and accessibility. Whether in the form of intermediate or final products, their maturity has probably been associated with an increasing and careful eye for quality. To the extent that the Philippines' product menu falls short of quality products relative to other countries in ASEAN, it will be difficult to maintain and increase market penetration, move up a product's value chain efficiently, and face more formidable obstacles outside the ASEAN markets where the Philippines supplies products that are similarly produced in the rest of the region.[5] The magnitude of this quality factor, especially in products that have matured, can be seen in the country's active participation in international standards bodies such as the International Organization for Standardization (ISO) and the Codex Alimentarius Commission, the number of testing and calibration laboratories, product certification bodies, and schemes offered by national accreditation bodies, among others.

A quick comparison of quality efforts among some of the ASEAN member states will show that the Philippines is behind Indonesia, Thailand, and Malaysia—and even Viet Nam on some benchmarks—reflecting poor quality infrastructure. Table 8.4 illustrates some of these indicators relative to Indonesia, Malaysia, Singapore, Thailand, and Viet Nam.

---

[5]   Of the many Philippine exports to ASEAN (which have been stable), some have gained dramatically in the last 5 years. These are mostly products that are differentiated and susceptible to quality differences, such as preparations of cereal, flour, starch, or milk; essential oils and/or perfumery; apparel and/or clothing accessories; and optical and photographic products.

Table 8.4: Illustrative Quality Indicators, 2011

	Indonesia	Malaysia	Philippines	Singapore	Thailand	Viet Nam
ISO (participation, no.)	225	280	121	150	295	79
Testing labs (no.)	541	344	17	238	368	479
Calibration labs (no.)	142	69	27	68	194	58
Schemes by NAB (no.)	11	11	9	12	10	8

ISO = International Organization for Standardization, NAB = National Accreditation Bodies.

Source: ASEAN Secretariat and country websites.

A country's active participation in ISO meetings involves the country's products in setting international standards, which are fulfilled by its testing and calibration laboratories. Table 8.4 shows that the Philippines lags behind Indonesia, Malaysia, and Thailand in this. While these comparisons are not clear-cut, since Indonesia too is an archipelago, it may be more appropriate. In this case, the Philippines is even farther behind.

Without attending to measures that would help in sustaining advances in market penetration, those products may lose competitiveness. Indeed, since many Philippine products have attained some maturity, increased readiness for quality-driven product differentiation will not only help retain market share but actually enlarge markets, since intra-industry trade accompanies increased economic growth. What is also true is that failure to attend to such readiness associated with product quality is also a strong basis for erecting nontariff barriers (e.g., health and sanitary standards, labeling requirements).

This readiness for maintaining if not enhancing markets in ASEAN does not only pertain to the region but to the rest of the world. After all, product improvements meant for the region can also be accessed by world markets, and vice versa.

The Philippine Mid-Term Review (MTR) of the AEC Blueprint notes that the country is progressing well toward ASEAN standards and conformance, especially among the eight priority investment sectors (Milo 2013; Aldaba et al. 2013). With regard to national obligations for standards, conformity assessments, and technical regulations, overall compliance rates are high. The numerical scorecard is based on the MTR Economic Research Institute for ASEAN and East Asia (ERIA) Survey of Core Measures, where (for the Philippines) 33 firms were surveyed to determine their awareness of the AEC and the degree of compliance with the measures. For the assessment of ASEAN standards and conformance along the eight priority sectors, the respondents were even fewer. For example, for cosmetics only seven were surveyed (five multinational firms, one small or medium-sized enterprise, and the Food and Drug Administration); in electronics only three were surveyed (one representing industry associations, one from the Bureau of Philippine Standards, and one from a laboratory). While the responses may reveal degrees of awareness and product standards, they are clearly quite incomplete. But these results are not inconsistent with the assertion underlying Table 8.4.

First of all, what is being evaluated in the MTR and in the standards and conformance part of the AEC under trade facilitation is adherence of products to minimum standards; that is, mandatory product properties intended to provide consumer protection and safety. This is often confused with product quality—indeed, this is the minimum that must be met by manufacturers and distributors.[6] This is what regulators are concerned with at the national level, while at the regional level harmonization of those mandatory requirements ensures that goods move faster and that they do not constitute technical barriers to trade.

Second, what is asserted above is that as product markets mature, consumers tend to look for quality. Quality standards are thus provided and driven by the private sector, but they require a quality infrastructure that is reflected by the illustrative indicators in Table 8.4. Laboratories aim for international compliance, allowing their certifications to be internationally recognized and accepted by private consumers. These are often beyond the mandatory technical standards and are initiated to satisfy quality requirements, which may lead to higher competitiveness, if not to price premiums that manufacturers can charge.

Third, the focus of the MTR and reported scorecard is compliance by manufacturers and traders with standards, conformity assessments, and technical requirements as imposed by regulators. Thus, the tables

---

[6] In the review of Philippine adherence to the ASEAN Cosmetic Directive, "... the harmonized technical requirements are readily available to the industry and both manufacturers and distributors appear to register high compliance with the essential requirements for product safety and quality..." (Milo 2013: 10–11, emphasis added).

underlying the scorecard for standards and conformance in the AEC relate to equivalence of national standards with agreed international and ASEAN standards, ratification of mutual recognition arrangements and their transposition into domestic laws, ratification of regional agreements containing harmonized technical regulations and regional post-market surveillance, among others (Aldaba et al. 2013, Tables 2.1–2.3). It is only appropriate to take this focus in fulfilling the country's obligations for the AEC.

Finally, it appears that the AEC measures for the Philippines (as well as the other ASEAN member states) are necessary conditions for integration, but, as argued here, they are not sufficient, especially in terms of sustaining what the country has gained from AFTA implementation. Indeed, where harmonization of standards and conformance is achieved, the challenge is for the private sector to move for quality standards to be competitive.

In summary, the Philippines is well within reach of its targets for the AEC's first pillar of a single market and production base, through trade in goods. However, if the ultimate test of its readiness is being able to sustain the momentum of its regional goods trade, its readiness is quite inadequate relative to the other member states. With respect to trade in services, foreign investment, and flows of capital and skilled labor, the country's readiness for the AEC is uneven—some requiring basic measures, some requiring regional approaches, and some requiring largely national efforts.

In services liberalization, the path to the AEC remains long and difficult. Although the pace of AFAS has quickened since the seventh round, and the Philippines has been adding more sectors for liberalization, the country's regional commitments hardly differ from its commitments under the WTO General Agreement on Trade in Services (GATS). Trade in a number of services may have significant returns of interest to the country (e.g., travel and related services, business process outsourcing, other business services), and where liberalization has been unilaterally pursued. In terms of regional interest, what is of immediate importance are services that remove barriers to movement of goods across countries. This would cover transport, logistics services, and freight forwarding, among others. Unfortunately, while ASEAN agreements on specific transport services liberalization have long been signed, these have not been ratified by all member states and thus remain unimplemented. For instance, the ASEAN Framework Agreement on Multimodal Transport, endorsed by the ASEAN Transport Ministers' Meeting in 2005, clearly recognized the need for multimodal transport operator to cross borders and to use at least two different modes of transport in the carriage of goods from a place in one country to a place designated for delivery in another country—meaning that the goods are taken in charge of only once by the transport operator (see Chapter 2). The same can be said of the ASEAN Framework Agreement on the Facilitation of Inter-State Transport, endorsed by the ASEAN Transport Ministers Meeting in 2009, which has yet to see ratification by the member states. Indeed, about 40 agreements, protocols, and memoranda of understanding related to transport (framework, land, air, maritime) have been signed not only among the ASEAN member states but with dialogue partners and the PRC. Less than 10 have entered into force. The readiness of the Philippines for trade-related ASEAN-centric services can partly be gauged by its ratification of important regional transport agreements even with continuing resistance to cabotage.

In investment and capital flows, the ratified ASEAN Comprehensive Investment Agreement (ACIA) enhances and supersedes the ASEAN Investment Area (AIA) and ASEAN Investment Guarantee agreements. And under the AEC, the aim of the free flow of investment and capital in the region is a liberal, facilitative, open, and competitive investment environment in ASEAN following international best practices. This means liberalized investment regimes in the ASEAN member states, and rules that facilitate, protect, and promote investments. Readiness of the Philippines for this ASEAN investment climate requires more national measures than regional efforts. In particular, there is a need to open up the economy to regional investments, especially in sectors that enhance the country's access to the global and regional markets. This will require removing constitutional limitations on ownership, harmonizing investment promotions policies that differ by investment promoting agency, paying full attention to basic and fundamental physical and institutional infrastructure (already ubiquitous in other member states), and ensuring compatibility of investment incentives with the rest of the region.[7]

With regard to liberalizing movement of skilled labor within ASEAN, individual member states need to jump several hurdles to integration. Even within one profession, there would be at most 10 different educational and training curricula with different courses and varying lengths of time. Although best practices may be available, the models may differ as well, such as between American or British systems. Then, there are varying

---

[7]   Various reviews by investment agencies of the ASEAN member states ensure there would be no "race to the bottom" through competing incentives to attract investments. Part of the AEC may have to address the tendency to outdo each other in giving incentives.

licensure requirements for the practice of professions. These are apart from different languages and cultural practices. ASEAN has resorted to a more systematic process of encouraging freer mobility of skilled labor: facilitation of visa issuances for business travelers; incentives for traders and investors; intra-corporate transferees (of multinational corporations in the region); professionals, including doctors, nurses, lawyers, engineers, accountants, information technology personnel, and other professions; a schedule of mutual recognition arrangements for the practice of professions, for which seven have been identified; development of core competencies and qualifications for skills required in the priority services sector; greater cooperation among ASEAN University Network members for staff and student mobility; and strengthened research in the ASEAN member states for promoting job skills and labor market information, among others.

However, having signed mutual recognition arrangements does not mean that the Philippines is ready for freer flow of skilled labor in the region. Although the country has been a net sender of skilled (and semi-skilled) labor to the rest of ASEAN, the AEC envisions mutual mobility, which means it will also have to be open to the inflow of professionals into the domestic labor market. This means the country undertakes procedures similar to the other member states, entailing the steps enumerated above. This will involve many government and private organizations responsible for the education and training of professionals, examining and licensing them to practice, reviewing curricula equivalences, matching fieldwork and training for some professions, and other qualifications. While some professional organizations are on their way to negotiating with counterparts in other countries on a bilateral basis (e.g., accountancy, although some member states still have to achieve a level of sophistication analogous to the Philippine Institute of Certified Public Accountants), others need a better understanding of what is involved to prepare the country for free mobility of professional skilled labor such as engineering, medical, and dental professions.

8.3   The Remaining ASEAN Economic Community Pillars

This section briefly examines the other elements of the AEC. We argue that although these other elements are important, they (i) hinge on trade in goods (in the single market and production base pillar), which will draw in services, investment, and labor movement; (ii) will require the combination of the three other AEC pillars, and (iii) will be instrumental for integration into the global economy including ASEAN.

All four pillars are integral parts of the AEC package (see Table 8.3). The remaining three pillars evolved out of the AEC road map but are nevertheless equally important for the AEC's realization. It is evident from Table 8.3, however, that the single market and production base pillar has the most number of agreements to support it. This is also where the Philippines is most ready in terms of a key component—trade in goods. We now turn to the country's readiness in terms of the three remaining pillars: competitive economic region, equitable economic development, and integration into the global economy.

Competitive Economic Region

International trade generally imposes market discipline (at least in the tradable sectors) and tends to diminish monopoly power in the domestic economy. But that discipline is limited, and competition policy is essential to overall competitiveness. The AEC Blueprint envisions competition policy in place in the member states by 2015. The Philippines has promulgated the new Philippine Competition Act, amending an interim Executive Order No. 45 creating the Office for Competition in the Department of Justice as the designated competition body. This will consolidate all the fragmented pieces of regulations and legislation that address restrictive business practices, price control, and unfair trade practices. At the same time, the dividing line between competition policy and regulation has to be clear under the new law to foster a competition environment. In the country, some government entities are both regulators and promoters of competition in such major sectors as telecommunication, electricity, ports, and air commerce.

The other tasks in the AEC are in consumer protection, intellectual property rights, infrastructure development, taxation, and e-commerce. There has been some progress in some of these (services related to infrastructure discussed above), indicating some readiness on the part of the country.

Equitable Economic Development

The third pillar of the AEC is meant to address the development divide in ASEAN and integrate the CLMV countries (Cambodia, Lao People's Democratic Republic, Myanmar, and Viet Nam) and focuses squarely on broad-based economic development. Regardless of how it is named—for example, "inclusive and resilient ASEAN" (Intal et al. 2014)—two action fronts are specified in the AEC Blueprint: development of SMEs and the Initiative for ASEAN Integration. The latter is systematic assistance from the ASEAN-6 for the integration of new members the rest of the member states. The former is an affirmative action to enhance the development of micro, small, and medium-sized enterprises in the region. The MTR of the Philippines' progress in the ASEAN Strategic Plan for SME Development and the ASEAN Policy Blueprint for SME Development shows low effectiveness in terms of access to finance, technology development, human resources development, and other regional SME concerns. However, these are not regional initiatives but national concerns that must be addressed at the national level. On the other hand, the Philippines continues to support and contribute assistance to the regional Initiative for ASEAN Integration and participates in seeking technical assistance from dialogue partners.

Integration into the Global Economy

With the AEC, ASEAN is envisioned to increasingly become integrated into the global economy while maintaining an "ASEAN centrality" in its external economic relations, especially in terms of concluding FTAs or regional economic cooperation arrangements. To achieve some coherence in ASEAN's external relations, the AEC Blueprint suggests actions toward common positions in regional and multilateral forums. A second direction is to support less developed member states and enhance their capability and productivity in participating in regional and global supply chain networks. This "ASEAN centrality" can be seen in the regional FTAs that have been negotiated, concluded, and ratified. Indeed, this pillar obtained the highest achievement rate of 85.7% on the AEC scorecard for its first two phases (2008–2011), measured by the entry into force of five FTAs (Australia and New Zealand, the PRC, India, Japan, and the Republic of Korea).

At the same time, the ASEAN member states negotiated bilateral FTAs with these same partners, covering items not in the ASEAN-centered FTAs such as movement of natural persons (Chia 2011). To the extent that the bilateral FTAs are with partners that also have FTAs with ASEAN, regional integration may be further strengthened. Given the limited number of collective FTAs, it is not surprising that the AEC scorecard for this pillar is high. On the other hand, since the ASEAN-centered FTAs also contain a schedule of products for tariff reduction, among other provisions, giving the fourth pillar a scorecard based simply on the entry into force of the FTA is not comparable to a scorecard for the first pillar, which goes into products and services trade. In the case of the ASEAN–Japan

Comprehensive Economic Partnership Agreement, each of the member states (and Japan) has a schedule of elimination on reduction of customs duties (Annex 1 of the agreement). For example, the Philippines has 223 pages of eight-digit Harmonized System (HS) products listed in the Annex 1 (to Article 16), which has 10 classification schedules using base tariff rates and their elimination to 0%–20% running into year 11 of the FTA (Japan Ministry of Foreign Affairs 2008). It is not clear how the country's readiness should be viewed for this ASEAN-centered FTA without referring to its MFN schedules, even if its intra-ASEAN rates would have been zero. Note also that from examining the ASEAN-centered FTA, it is not clear how differing schedules laid out by each member state lead to an enriched regional economy. The individual FTAs have the potential to raise trade (and investment) bilaterally and, when combined with ASEAN-level FTAs, regional trade (and investment). As noted earlier, these will depend on how the regional FTAs have been formulated.

8.4   Concluding Remarks

Of the four pillars underlying the AEC, our focus in this chapter has been on the single market and production base—and within this, trade in goods. This is not to deny the importance of the other pillars, or the other components of the first pillar—that is, the flow of services, investment, capital, and skilled labor. Trade in goods, however, has had the longest tracking of regional trade since it began with AFTA (theoretically even earlier with preferential trade). It also has the largest number of core agreements. This chapter has shown that during the period of AFTA implementation, the Philippines did not only aggressively pursue a program of preferential tariff reduction but a concomitant reduction of MFN tariff rates. Between 1993 and 1999, the margins between Philippine AFTA rates and its MFN rates sharply declined, so that the initial preferential bias in terms of both exports to and imports from ASEAN diminished (see Figure 8.1) and trade shares with the region remained stable. As Calvo-Pardo, Freund, and Ornelas (2009) have argued, the simultaneous decline in both CEPT and MFN rates improved welfare, minimized trade diversion, and increased trade creation. While it is difficult to disentangle the contribution of either, we posit that the country's readiness for the AEC was already laid down at the start of AFTA and fortified when it unilaterally liberalized on an MFN basis. This is only one part, albeit a critical one, of the AEC package. The other pillars and the other parts of the first pillar are still beset by barriers to effective regional trade. These are mostly homegrown and putting the house in order is necessary not only for the AEC but for firmer integration with the world economy. Even with the current progress in trade in goods, sustaining this requires a readiness that requires attention—with or without the AEC. On the other hand, the AEC itself could be a strong incentive for the Philippines to carry out the necessary reforms—the country's ASEAN commitments pressure it to continue on its reform path.

The literature on the AEC and related ASEAN initiatives is staggeringly voluminous. Many of them tout ASEAN as an icon of regional integration and cooperation, which would be true. They make it appear as if the world is all ASEAN and that the community is there.[8] The more sober of the literature is more cautious, declaring that the AEC is not an end but a milestone, and warning that the AEC targets are not likely to be met as scheduled (Menon 2014; Hill and Menon 2010).[9] Most of the papers detail regional readiness for the AEC as reflected in the monitoring system in place such as the number of measures implemented relative to the total measures committed (e.g., showing an 84.1% implementation rate for the Philippines).

A way to argue for this readiness is by first identifying the weaknesses in a particular area of regional competition through comparative analysis. Then, a specific measure is proposed as a policy direction meant to strengthen the country in the coming AEC. For example, if the Philippines is weak in science and technology such as in research and development (R&D) and public funding of education, which results in uncompetitive products and migration of skills, a solution is to increase support to R&D, provide performance-based resources for selected higher educational institutions, and link tertiary education to industry (Pernia and Clarete 2014). But these measures are neutral and their effects may be on ASEAN but may also be on the rest of the world.[10] This is analogous to the simultaneous decline in both CEPT and MFN rates during AFTA, in part explaining the low submission of forms to make use of lower CEPT rates. Did this mean poor progress of ASEAN, AFTA, or the AEC? Not necessarily. They may have instead been

---

[8]   Other than government bureaucrats, some businesses, and limited regional organizations, the general public in ASEAN is not aware of the AEC or even ASEAN. Surprisingly, in one survey of manufacturers and traders the number of respondents who are not aware of the AEC is highest in Singapore (Hu 2013).

[9]   Included in this is probably the lengthy document ASEAN Rising: ASEAN and the AEC Beyond 2015, which admits that AEC targets were unmet, but appropriately maintains ASEAN as the primordial star in regional integration (Intal et al. 2014).

[10]   In terms of the AEC, this can always be catered to through such means as the ASEAN University Network or faculty and staff and/or student exchanges, in which case first movers would come from ASEAN (assuming the outputs respond to these AEC measures).

welfare-improving for the country. Indeed, narrowing measures only for ASEAN and/or the AEC necessarily "locks-in" the country to the region. In the increasing globalization of production and consumption, where it may be impossible to capture let alone identify segments of the value chain (that ASEAN can indefinitely hold), the forgone opportunities may be more significant at this time than during the early period of AFTA.

A remaining argument for preparing for the AEC rather than more neutrally for the world is that it forces us to undertake reforms, gear policies for the coming wider markets, and work to attract (regional) investment and capital. This is an appealing point suggesting that concentrating on the single market pillar, particularly on trade in goods (and eventually services), will also influence the environment for investments, capital, and movement of labor. After all, dynamic trade in regional and global markets ultimately dictates product location, the ensuing associated capital and investments, and the flow of particular labor. Neighbors may be the first to benefit from such dynamism, but so would the world at large.

Of the original five ASEAN members, most have successfully overcome barriers to integration into the regional and global trade and investment systems. Thus, for some of these countries, aggressive pursuit of the AEC is marginal and a by-product of global readiness. Their respective institutional machinery has been built around the global trading arena, their economic actors exploit border opportunities, their governments are bold in forging agreements that open markets. The Philippines has yet to fully be ready for the global market, its economic actors still have to appreciate borders and their potential for expanding markets, and its government carries out audacious reforms that realize its nearby neighbors can be exploited as part of the larger world economy.

References

Alburo, F. 1995. AFTA in the Light of New Economic Developments. In D. Singh and L.T. Kiat, eds. *Southeast Asian Affairs 1995.* Singapore: Institute of Southeast Asian Studies.

Aldaba, R., et al. 2013. The ASEAN Economic Community and the Philippines: Implementation, Outcomes, Impacts, and Ways Forward. ERIA Research Project. *PIDS Discussion Paper* 2013-01 (January 2013). Makati: Philippine Institute for Development Studies.

ASEAN Secretariat. 1976. *The Declaration of ASEAN Concord, Bali, Indonesia, 24 February 1976*. Jakarta.

———. 2005a. *ASEAN Framework Agreement on Multi-Modal Transport.* Jakarta: ASEAN Secretariat.

———. 2005b. Initiative for ASEAN Integration: Work Plan for the CLMV Countries, Progress Report as at 15 May 2005. Jakarta: ASEAN Secretariat.

———. 2007a. ASEAN Community Progress Monitoring System (ACPMS): Pan-ASEAN Indicators, Measuring Progress towards the ASEAN Economic Community and the ASEAN Socio-Cultural Community Volume 1. Jakarta: ASEAN Secretariat.

———. 2007b. ASEAN Community Progress Monitoring System (ACPMS): Country Indicators and Monitoring Tools, Measuring Progress towards the ASEAN Economic Community and the ASEAN Socio-Cultural Community Volume 2. Jakarta: ASEAN Secretariat.

———. 2008. *ASEAN Economic Community Blueprint.* Jakarta: ASEAN Secretariat.

———. 2009. ASEAN Framework Agreement on the Facilitation of Inter-State Transport. Jakarta.

———. 2010a. *Table of ASEAN Treaties/Agreements and Ratification* (as of April 2010). Jakarta.

———. 2010b. *ASEAN Economic Community Scorecard.* Jakarta, Indonesia: ASEAN Secretariat. March 2010. Jakarta.

———. 2012. *ASEAN Economic Community Scorecard.* March 2012. Jakarta.

Calvo-Pardo, H., C. Freund, and E. Ornelas. 2009. The ASEAN Free Trade Agreement: Trade Flows and External Trade Barriers. *CEP Discussion Paper* 930. London: Centre for Economic Performance London School of Economics and Political Science.

Chia, S.Y. 2004. Economic Cooperation and Integration in East Asia. *Asia-Pacific Review* (May 2004): 1–19.

————. 2011. Free Flow of Skilled Labor in AEC. In S. Urata and M. Okabe, eds. *Toward a Competitive ASEAN Single Market: Sectoral Analysis.* ERIA Research Project 2010-03. Jakarta: Economic Research Institute for ASEAN and East Asia. pp. 205–279.

Cuyvers, L., P. De Lombaerde, and S. Verherstraeten. 2005. From AFTA Towards an ASEAN Economic Community…and Beyond. *Center for ASEAN Studies Discussion Paper* No. 46. Patumthani, Thailand: Center for ASEAN Studies.

Habito, C. 2014. The ASEAN Economic Community and the Philippine Economy. NCC Dialogues, Asian Institute of Management. 26 June.

Hill, H., and J. Menon. 2010. ASEAN Economic Integration: Features, Fulfillments, Failures and the Future' *ADB Working Paper Series on Regional Economic Integration No. 69.* Manila: Asian Development Bank.

Hu, A. 2013. The ASEAN Economic Community Business Survey. in S. Das, et al. eds. *The ASEAN Economic Community: A Work in Progress.* Manila and Singapore: Asian Development Bank and Institute of Southeast Asian Studies.

Intal, P. Jr. et al. 2014. *ASEAN Rising: ASEAN and AEC Beyond 2015.* Jakarta: Economic Research Institute for ASEAN and East Asia.

Government of Japan, Japan Ministry of Foreign Affairs. 2008. *ASEAN-Japan Comprehensive Economic Partnership Agreement.* Tokyo.

Krugman, P. 2011. Can Europe Be Saved? *New York Times.* 12 January.

Menon, J. 2014. Moving Too Slowly towards ASEAN Economic Community. *East Asia Forum.* 14 October. http://www.eastasiaforum.org/2014/10/14/moving-too-slowly-towards-an-asean-economic-community/.

Milo, M. 2013. The ASEAN Economic Community and the Philippines: Implementation, Outcomes, Impacts, and Ways Forward. *PIDS Research Paper Series* No. 2013-02. Makati: Philippine Institute for Development Studies.

Mundell, R.A. 1961. A Theory of Optimum Currency Areas. *American Economic Review* 51(4): 657–665.

Nandan, G. 2006. *ASEAN: Building an Economic Community.* Canberra, Australia: Department of Foreign Affairs and Trade, Economic Analytical Unit.

Pernia, E., and R. Clarete. 2014. Investing in S&T and R&D in Face of AEC Competition. *PCED Policy Notes* 2014-04 (May 2014). Quezon City: Philippine Center for Economic Development.

Schirru. G. 2014. Europe's Other Languages. *East Global Geopolitics* No. 53 (May-June): 24–25.

Society for the Advancement of Technology Management in the Philippines (SATMP). 2003. A Study on the Measurement of the Time Required for the Release of Goods in the Philippines. Report submitted to the Bureau of Customs and Japan International Cooperation Agency.

Forging ahead together. The adoption of the Kuala Lumpur Declaration on ASEAN 2025 at the 27th ASEAN Summit held in November 2015 underscores ASEAN's continued commitment to pursuing regional integration (photo from the ASEAN Secretariat Photo Archives).

INDEX

Figures, notes, and tables are indicated by "f," "n," and "t" following page numbers. Illustrations are indicated by page numbers in italics.

CPSIA information can be obtained
at www.ICGtesting.com
Printed in the USA
BVHW021241191119
R10454200002B/R104542PG563684BVX15B/1/P